THE MINISTER: HIS WORLD AND HIS WORK

THE MINISTER
HIS WORLD AND
HIS WORK

A Study of
Some Pressing Tasks and Problems
of Present-Day Protestantism

By
WILLIAM ADAMS BROWN, Ph.D.
D.D., S.T.D.

COKESBURY PRESS
NASHVILLE, TENN.

SET UP, ELECTROTYPED, PRINTED
AND BOUND BY THE PARTHENON
PRESS AT NASHVILLE, TENNESSEE
UNITED STATES OF AMERICA

C

PREFACE

AT the outset a word of explanation is due to the reader as to why I, who have already written three books about the Church, should add a fourth. When, a few months ago, I received an invitation to address two groups of Southern ministers in Texas, nothing was farther from my thought than that what I then said should find its way into print; but the cordial reception which I there received and the intimation coming to me from many quarters that my way of putting what I had to say might be helpful to my hearers if preserved in book form—an intimation which culminated in a formal request for publication from both groups—has led me to reconsider my original intention.

Two further motives have influenced me, without which even the warmth of this request might not have persuaded me. In the first place, I am keenly aware that, in spite of all our talk about Christian co-operation and unity, there still remains a wide gap between the world in which the average parish minister is living and the plans of those who are leaders in the movement for Christian unity in the Church-at-large. It has seemed to me, therefore, that a book on the practical problems which the Church is facing today which would approach its subject not primarily from the point of view of what the leaders are planning and saying but from the point of view of what the parish minister is thinking and doing might fill a needed gap.

One further hope has influenced me. It is that the line

of thought which the lectures follow may suggest to those
who are responsible for the Church's leadership ways in
which the wider insights to which their more extensive experience has brought them may be more definitely related
to the task which the local minister faces in the individual
parish and congregation. It is the parish minister who,
in the last analysis, must be interpreter to his people of
the function of the Church in our modern world. I believe that those who are responsible for the leadership of the
Church both in the denomination and in the Church-at-
large have been too easily content with holding up before
the ministry an ideal which, however inspiring, presents
difficulties of application of almost overwhelming magnitude. They have not sufficiently realized their responsibility for assembling the information and sharing the experience which would help the minister to point out to his
people ways in which the great ideal which he holds up to
them can be translated from dream into fact.

I make no apology, therefore, for retaining in the
printed page the simple and informal mode of address
which I have followed in my lectures. In other books,
notably my books on *Pathways to Certainty* and *Church
and State in Contemporary America,* I have developed in
some detail lines of thought at which I have been able
here only to hint. When passages from these books seemed
likely to be helpful I have not hesitated to use them. But
my main purpose has not been to write a learned book,
but as one Christian minister talking to others about the
tasks and problems which confront us all, to share whatever insight and experience nearly half a century of service

in the cause of the unity of Christ's Church may have given me with those upon whose shoulders the heaviest responsibility for the Church's work rests, and must ever rest.

Five of the lectures which are here reprinted were delivered at the School of Theology of the Southern Methodist University of Dallas, Texas, in February, 1937. They were repeated the following week, with the addition of two others, the third and fourth of the present series, at the Texas Ministers' Institute of Brite College of the Bible, at Texas Christian University at Fort Worth. To make possible a somewhat fuller treatment than was practicable in the time available the last two lectures have been divided and appear as Chapters VI-IX of the present book.

The material included in Chapters III, IV, and V was given in somewhat expanded form as the Rehrig Foundation Lectures at Muhlenberg College at Allentown, Pennsylvania, in November, 1936. Part of the material in Lecture VII was given to a group of Congregational ministers in September, 1920.

For the courtesy extended to me by all who made possible these lectureships I wish to express my cordial thanks.

My thanks are due to Messrs. Charles Scribner's Sons for allowing me to reproduce certain passages from two recent books of mine, *Pathways to Certainty* and *Church and State in Contemporary America*. I have also used a few paragraphs from an older book, *Is Christianity Practicable?* also published by Scribner's.

TABLE OF CONTENTS

[9]

CONTENTS

CONTENTS

CHAPTER I

THE WORLD IN WHICH THE MINISTER MUST DO HIS WORK

1. THE DOUBLE SETTING OF THE MINISTER'S WORK

2. THE MINISTER AS MAN OF THE WORLD

3. THE MINISTER AS MAN OF GOD

4. NEW FACTORS IN THE WORLD TODAY

5. IN WHAT SENSE WE FACE A WORLD CRISIS

Chapter I

1. THE DOUBLE SETTING OF THE MINISTER'S WORK

I AM to talk to you about some of the living issues which face the Protestant minister of today. These issues are not new. They deal with the perennial themes of human need and divine salvation. But they come to us in a new setting and make special demands upon the minister who would meet them with an open mind. My excuse for coming to you is that my work during the past few years has taken me to many countries and brought me into touch with many leaders of the Church, both in our own country and across the sea. I hope, therefore, that I may be able to put these old questions in the larger setting in which they meet us in this confused and troubled world in which we are living today.

It is one of the perplexing, and yet fascinating, aspects of the minister's profession that he is a man who is living in two worlds. So far as his physical structure and antecedents are concerned, he is a child of nature, subject to all the limitations of life in the body. Like all his fellows, he is a creature of time and space, dependent for the communication of his thought upon language, with all the possibilities of misunderstanding which that implies. But at the same time he is a child of the eternal, conscious of living in a divine world, of which all that can be conveyed through sense is but a symbol. He believes that there is a real God who has commerce with men, and that it is possible for us to know him. And he further believes that through Jesus Christ and the long line of history that leads up to him, and that other line that leads from him in uninterrupted succession down to our own day, we have a trustworthy knowledge of God's purpose for us and for our world. That long line of revelation coming to us across the centuries we sum up in the words "Bible and Church." But all that it means it would take more chapters than our schedule allows to unfold.

This dual aspect of the minister's life as a child of nature and a recipient of revelation is reflected in the social institutions through which his life is lived. He is a minister of the Church. And the Church differs from all other human institutions in that its primary concern is with religion. Its specialty is worship. And worship is the way in which finite man affirms and expresses his relation to the infinite and eternal. In prayer, we creatures of time and change lay hold upon the realities that outlast change and realize that our true citizenship is in heaven.

But the Church is not the only institution to which the minister belongs and in which he must live his life. He is man of the world as well as man of God, and this second world in which his life is lived—the world we often call secular—is a social world as well. It expresses itself through a variety of institutions: the family, the school, the economic order, above all the state. To all these the minister belongs and with all these he has to do. He is citizen as well as churchman, husband and father as well as minister, teacher as well as evangelist and leader in worship. And this dual relationship sets him all sorts of tasks and involves him in all sorts of problems for which no ready-made solution seems possible.

For the past six years I have been engaged, in association with a group of representative Christians appointed by the Federal Council, in a study of the relation of church and state in contemporary America.[1] This study has revealed to us how perplexing these problems are. I have said that the minister is living in two worlds, the supernatural world and the natural world. But when we try to map the geography of the two worlds and define their boundaries we find that they overlap in surprising and baffling ways. We speak of the Church as a divine institution—the custodian of the divine revelation and redemption; but when we contemplate the Church as it meets us in the world today we find that it is a very human institution, with all the limitations and imperfections of our humanity. Theologians define the Church as one, holy, apostolic, and catholic. But when we ask where we are to find evidence of these qualities, the results are disappointing. Instead of one Church, we find many: Protestant and Catholic, Presbyterian and Methodist, Lutheran and Con-

[1] Brown, W. Adams, *Church and State in Contemporary America*, New York, 1936.

gregationalist, Baptist and Disciples. And even these are divided and subdivided in ways that tax the ingenuity of the Church historian to explain.

Instead of a holy church, without spot or wrinkle or any such thing, as the New Testament describes it, we see a church made up of imperfect and sinful men, who act, and, what is still more serious, who judge, very much as their fellows in school and state act and judge.

We speak of the Church as apostolic. But if we could bring back the Apostle Paul to life and take him for a tour of our American churches, he would not know how to reconcile their imposing edifices and, still more, their imposing bank accounts with the primitive simplicity of that Corinthian church of which he wrote: "For ye see your calling, brethren, how that not many wise men after the flesh, not many mighty, not many noble, are called." [2]

And as for catholicity, how far the Church is from being universal we realize when we reflect that not only are there whole countries where Christianity is still only the religion of a minority, but that in our own day one of the greatest of all the so-called Christian countries, Russia, has definitely rejected Christianity.

Nor are the perplexities all on one side, for if we find the marks of limitation and imperfection present in the Church, which claims to have a monopoly of the divine, it is equally true that the institutions we are in the habit of calling secular refuse to remain within the limits to which we have assigned them. They, too, are conscious of spiritual meanings and responsibilities. They, too, call forth

[2] 1 Corinthians 1: 26.

[18]

loyalties that outlast time and change. They, too, may be objects of a devotion that can only be described as religious.

Take the most familiar and intimate of all human institutions, the family. From the point of view of the state, the family is a civil institution into which one enters by a contract enforceable (or dissoluble) by law. It has its physical aspects and responsibilities which have their analogy in the life of other members of the animal kingdom. But no one who has married for love will believe for a moment that these aspects of the family exhaust its significance. To the devout Catholic marriage is a sacrament—that is, an outward sign of an inward and spiritual grace. And while Protestants, for reasons easily to be understood historically, no longer speak of marriage as a sacrament in the technical sense, they are just as convinced as their Catholic fellow Christians that marriage is a divine institution with which we play fast and loose at our peril. There is an unseen factor to be taken into account: God, who instituted the marriage relation to be a channel not only of physical life but of spiritual grace. "What God hath joined together," so run the solemn words, "let not man put asunder." [3]

What is true of marriage is true in greater or less degree of all other human institutions. They are not simply legal devices to enable men and women to live together without quarreling and perform their functions more effectively than they could do if they were living in isolation. They have spiritual meaning as the channels through

[3] Mark 10: 9.

which the divine life to which man is called expresses itself in its social manifestations. This was the great truth for which the Reformation stood, the truth of the sacredness of the secular, or as we may put it in another form, of the universal priesthood of believers. There is no calling, so our Protestant forefathers believed, but may be made a divine ministry. School as well as church, commerce as well as preaching, may be ways in which the Christian man confesses his dependence upon God and consecrates his life to his service.

What is true of family and school and business is no less true of that human institution which is most commonly contrasted with the Church as secular, the state. "From the point of view of the sociologist the state means the political community. It is the inclusive social unit through which, within a definite territory, the community makes and enforces law. Narrowly defined, it is the institution or institutions through which this political function is discharged. Broadly speaking, it is the group of people who live under this institution and accept its authority." [4]

But no one who knows what it means to live in a particular state, whether that state be Germany or England or France or the United States, will believe for a moment that such a purely sociological definition can exhaust all that his citizenship means to him. To any sincere patriot the state no less than the Church is a spiritual reality, reminding him of eternal verities which give it a claim upon his devotion and loyalty. No merely secular institution can explain the thrill we feel when on Independence Day we sing

[4] *Church and State in Contemporary America* (New York, 1936), p. 32.

"My country, 'tis of thee,
Sweet land of liberty,"

or on Thanksgiving Day, at the summons of the President, we meet in church to render thanks to God for the blessings of the year. No merely secular institution could have the right to ask the sacrifice which, when the call of the Great War came, emptied our colleges of the flower of our youth to serve in a distant land, if need be at the cost of their lives.

The problem then of drawing the line between church and state, between the religious and the secular, is not an easy one. For church and state, as we meet them in the world today, are not two independent entities standing over against each other, each striving for the mastery. They are differing aspects of a single society made up of people both political and religious. It is true that for reasons which are easily explicable historically the state is more inclusive than the Church. There are citizens, whether they are increasing in numbers or not it is not easy to say, who are not members of any church. Nevertheless, the area of common membership is so great as to constitute a very real problem.

2. THE MINISTER AS MAN OF THE WORLD

It is this dual relationship to the church on the one hand, to the group of institutions we commonly call secular on the other, which sets the minister his peculiar problem. He is a citizen of two countries. Yet in his heart he knows that in the mind of God they were meant to be one,

[21]

and it is his task to help them to achieve that unity. It is not his task to win men to the Church as an institution already perfect and holy, any more than it is his task to denounce business and the state as institutions wholly evil. It is his task to use the resources of divine grace open to him in the great tradition of which the Church is custodian, to win men, whether in business, state, or church, to the type of life Christ our Master would approve. To suggest how this may be done in the confused and perplexing environment in which we find ourselves today is the primary purpose of these studies.

It will help us if we can be clear at the outset as to what the minister's distinctive function and mission is. What, in the first place, we may ask, must the minister do which other men who are ministers are not doing? Let us begin by listing some of the duties he has in common with other men.

In the first place, the minister is a family man. If he is unmarried, he is son and brother; if he is married, he is husband and father; and all the problems which grow out of life in the family are his problems, not only in the sense that as a public teacher he has an interest in their solution, but in the sense that they are his personal problems, and if he cannot solve them rightly for himself he cannot hope to help others.

In the next place the minister is a man of business. Not, to be sure, in the sense in which we sometimes use the word, that he is engaged in some branch of industry which has for its primary purpose what we call the making of money, but in the sense that he is a part of the social and industrial order in which we live and that he cannot perform the simplest of his daily functions—ordering the dinner, paying the bills, renting a hall, building a church—without being plunged into the heart of the economic problems which are under debate between the capitalist and the socialist and all the intermediate groups that lie between.

In the next place the minister is a teacher. What and how he is to teach will concern us in a later chapter. It is sufficient here to say that his work as teacher, whether we think of it in the more general way in which it is performed through the pulpit or in its more technical form as teacher of Bible class or Sunday school, brings him into the heart of the educational world as that world meets us in our colleges and schools and confronts him with all its perplexing problems. How to tell the difference between fact and guesswork, how to share insights when reached, how far to rely on authority as a method of transmitting knowledge, where and how far to appeal to individual initiative: all these problems of the teacher the minister meets every day, and this fact makes him a member of the guild of teachers with all their dignities and responsibilities.

Once more, the minister is a citizen. He is a member of the political community and as such not only subject to the state, where the state has a right to command, but responsible as voter and molder of public opinion for the shaping of policies to which the state is committed. It is not optional with him whether he shall go into politics. He is in politics by the very fact of his status as an American citizen. The only question open to him is whether he shall go out of politics by refusing to exercise his function as a citizen, and so a molder of public opinion; or, granting that he accepts that responsibility, how he shall discharge it aright.

In all these things the minister is a man like other men. He is and must in the nature of the case be in the truest sense of that word a man of the world. But at the same time he must be a minister of the gospel. And that means a man of God. What exactly do we mean by that term?

3. THE MINISTER AS MAN OF GOD

When we say that the minister must be a man of God we do not mean that it is his duty in any of these other relations that we have described to be more religious than his neighbors. They, too, like him, are children of God, and it is their duty, as it is his, to live as fathers, husbands, citizens, teachers, men of business, in a way that Christ would approve. But we do mean that in addition to these other functions which he shares with them the minister has a special function which gives his calling distinction: that of leading people in the public worship of God and of helping them to the knowledge and the attitude that will enable them to take part in that worship intelligently and acceptably.

I say it is the minister's distinctive function to lead people in the public worship of God. Worship, to be sure, is no monopoly either of minister or church. It is not only open to every one, but it is every one's duty and privilege to practice it. "Pray without ceasing" is a text which recognizes no distinction of office, and the experience of a saint like Brother Lawrence shows that it is as possible to pray while performing the most menial tasks in kitchen or office as when attending the formal services of the Church.

But it is a well-known psychological law that a power that is not used easily becomes atrophied. We need, therefore, some stated reminder of the duty and privilege of worship, and this reminder is provided by the services of the Church. The Church is not the only institution that worships, but it is the only institution whose *specialty* is worship. And the minister, if he is a true minister, shares this characteristic of the institution he serves. He is the man who leads the people in the public worship of God and so helps them to make vivid to themselves what it means to have a God who is real and to draw the consequences which follow for conduct.

During the period between the signing of the Armistice and the return of the troops to the different countries from which they had come, the United States Government conducted a school for the soldiers who were still on foreign soil. In this school they studied things which would be helpful to them in their future business or profession. Among other subjects the ministry was included, and some of us, who, as members of the General War-Time Commission of the Churches, had been close to the government, were asked to prepare plans for this section of the school. We were anxious, therefore, to find such literature as was available on the claim of the ministry as a profession, and we scanned the accessible prewar material with an eagle eye to see what we could find. One address stood out above all the others as useful for our purpose. It was an address delivered by Woodrow Wilson to college students when he was still a professor at Princeton.

I happened to stand at his side on the platform when that address was delivered, and I remember as vividly as if it were yesterday a question that was asked him and how he answered it. "How ought a minister to dress, professor?" he was asked. "Should he wear clerical dress, or just ordinary clothes?" Quick as a flash came the answer: "It makes no difference what the minister wears. But one thing matters supremely. He should never be in any company of men for a single instant without making them realize that they are in the company of a minister of religion."

That, I think, puts the question of the relation of the two worlds in a nutshell. The minister is to be at home in every institution, but he is never to leave any one for a moment in doubt that he is first of all a man of God, a minister of the gospel.

This affects all the other things that the minister does. It affects his life in the family. It affects his teaching. It affects his work as man of business and as citizen. He is to be an example in every one of these relations of the kind of man a Christian ought to be.

What this means in detail we shall consider in later lectures. Here we are concerned for the moment with the question of the kind of world in which the minister is living, the kind of problem it sets for the man who in its confused and many-sided life desires to live as a man of God.

[26]

4. NEW FACTORS IN THE WORLD TODAY

It is a commonplace today to say that the Church is facing a crisis. I want for a moment to ask you to consider with me what this statement means and how it bears upon our work as ministers.

There is a sense in which the Church is always facing a crisis. Always it is confronted with the world-old struggle between good and evil, sin and salvation. You can dip into the memoirs of the wise men of every generation, from the days of ancient Egypt down to our own, and you will find them lamenting that the world is facing a crisis. The old ways are falling into disrepute and the young people are no longer ready to heed the wisdom of their elders.

I remember reading in one of Disraeli's letters a comment on the young women of the Mid-Victorian Era. "The trouble with them," he tells us, "is that they wear their skirts too short and they are too free with men."

It is not of such recurrent facts that I am thinking now, but of such new factors as may have entered into the life of our time as justify us in setting it apart from the ages that have preceded it as confronting us with quite peculiar and exceptional problems.

That there is such a new factor I believe no thoughtful man will deny. That new factor is modern science, and this both in its capacity as pure science, affecting man's ways of thinking, and in its capacity of applied science, affecting his ways of acting.

It is difficult to tell which of these two aspects has been

most revolutionary in its effects, for they play into one another in surprising and unexpected ways. You can make a good case for either. But I am inclined to believe that it is in its capacity as pure science that the effects of the change that has been taking place in our habits during the past half century will be shown to be most far-reaching.

For what has been happening to the world in the period of which I am speaking is not so much a change in specific beliefs, unbelievably great as that change has been, as in the general temper of mind with which the younger generation approaches all questions of belief. The old attitude of unquestioning acceptance of authority which was characteristic of the age in which some of the older ones of us began our life is gone, and we live in an age in which the dominating note is uncertainty.

This is reflected in the tone of our academic life. The old education was founded upon religion. Today in many of our great universities—the free universities of the East, as well as the state universities of the West—religion is either banished altogether or regarded as an elective which one may take or not as one pleases.

But the revolutionary effects of the modern scientific spirit appear not only in the breakdown of the old authorities, but in the accentuation of the problems which cry out for solution. And here applied science is contributing its share to the passing of old landmarks. Compare a modern factory with the type of shop that produced the goods that went to clothe and feed our fathers, or for that matter the modern farm. Compare with the ships in which Nelson fought the French at Trafalgar a single modern battleship. You could rebuild Yale University from the ground up for the price of one of these; and its life, if all goes well, will not extend beyond ten years.

Science has not only accelerated speed, it has annihilated space. It has brought East and West together, and with the rapprochement it has brought to birth a host of new problems which affect your life and mine in unforeseeable ways. Japan becomes industrialized and begins to undersell American products. Germany loses her colonies and has no access to raw materials. And the lesson is burned into us as with letters of fire that nations, like individuals, are members one of another; that if we cannot help one another to a peaceful solution of our problems, we shall find war knocking at our doors.

We hear a great deal today of the efforts that are being made in Washington to draft an ironclad neutrality law that will keep us out of the next world war. Let us hope that such efforts will succeed. But let us not be under any illusion. For two and one-half years Woodrow Wilson tried with all his distinguished resources and ability to keep us out of the last world war, and he failed in the end. For there are forces stronger than self-interest, and these are the passions of men. God grant that it may not prove so again.

It is this jostling of the nations against one another in a world which modern science has brought together, while at the same time it has undermined the old authorities that made men contented with their lot; it is this revolutionary change which explains the distinctive feature of the world of our time—the rise of the totalitarian state.

"By the totalitarian state we do not mean simply a state which in certain contingencies exercises the power of life and death, for that is a power which the state has always possessed under certain conditions. We do not mean a state that claims to rule by divine right within the sphere that is appropriate for government. For that is a right which in the past has been freely conceded to the state by the Church. We mean a state that aspires to control all phases of the life of man: his cultural, his economic, his religious, as well as his political life. We mean a state that claims to be not only the rightful, but the supreme, object of loyalty; a state which can tolerate the Church, if at all, only as a servant, never as an equal, still less as a superior." [5]

This is something new under the sun. There have been times in past history when church and state have struggled for the mastery both in individual countries and in Christendom as a whole. But they have been struggles within a single civilization by persons who both claimed to accept the Christian revelation and who differed only in their understanding of its meaning. Today the issue we face is far more radical, for it concerns the authority of the Christian revelation itself. In Russia that authority is uncompromisingly rejected. Religion, we are told, is the opiate of the people, beguiling them by the promise of

[5] Brown W. Adams, *Church and State in Contemporary America* (New York, 1936), p. 12.

happiness after death to present acceptance of preventable evils. It is to science, not religion, that we are to look for salvation, and the state which is responsible for the education of the oncoming generation has declared war upon religion in the name of science. While in theory it allows the individual the privilege of personal religion, officially it gives its blessing to the atheistic propaganda which is gathering its millions into the Society of the Godless.

In Germany, to be sure, where the doctrine of the totalitarian state has been carried out even more consistently than in Russia, the anti-Christian character of its present policy is not so frankly confessed. Unlike Communism, the Germany of Hitler professes to be Christian. Indeed it bases its chief claim to recognition on the fact that it has saved Germany from Communism. But it has done this at the price of the surrender of two fundamental characteristics of Christianity: its universalism and the central position it gives to love—in God and in man.[6]

This surrender is made explicitly by the representatives of that pagan tribal religion which is the real faith which inspires the leaders of National Socialism today. Writers like Rosenberg and Frau Ludendorff have no word but of scorn for internationalism in any of its forms. If Rosenberg still claims Jesus as authority for his gospel of blood and soil, it is because he has made him over into the image of a Teutonic chieftain, the apostle of courage as opposed to pity, and of pride as opposed to humility. Other more radical exponents of the new faith do not feel the neces-

[6] In this and the following pages I have used some paragraphs from my book, *Church and State in Contemporary America.* Cf. pp. 10, 11, 14, 18, 19.

sity for this redressing of an outworn hero. They are ready to break with Christianity completely, and to replace the God of Christianity by a militant deity more congenial to the temper of the party in power.

It is true that official Germany disavows these extreme positions. But where its sympathy really lies appears from the fact that it requires of all parties complete support of the decrees of the state and that it excludes from equal rights in the Church and in the state the members of that race which gave us the Old Testament and to which our Lord himself belonged.

What we see in Russia and in Germany is only the clearest illustration of tendencies which are widespread in the world today. Wherever we look we see the state assuming new responsibility and claiming new obedience. We might have chosen our illustrations from Italy, or from Mexico, or from Turkey, in all of which we see the state assuming new responsibilities and limiting the activities of the Church in fields where it has hitherto been regarded as supreme. We might have chosen our illustration from Japan, where Christians are being required, as a test of loyalty, to bow at Shinto shrines, thus raising the very issue which in the days before the conversion of Constantine made the choice between Christ and Caesar for many an early Christian a matter of life or death.

5. IN WHAT SENSE WE FACE A WORLD CRISIS

We are ready now to answer in a more definite way the question raised tentatively at an earlier point in the chapter: how far and in what sense the Church is facing a world crisis. The answer is that the Church is facing such a crisis because the issues which divide men today are not only political and economic but religious. What we see is a transfer of loyalties. Forces which we have hitherto regarded as religious in the technical sense—the longing for authority, the need of salvation, the sense of solidarity, the capacity for sacrifice—all of them factors which have played their majestic rôle in the history of Christianity: these forces we see today redirected to a new object of loyalty—the state.

It is not only in autocratic countries like Russia and Germany that this growing power of the state is to be recognized. Christopher Dawson, that brilliant English Roman Catholic essayist, has shown us in a recent book how the modern state may use the forms of democratic government in order to enforce its control over the whole of life. "What modern Christians have to fear from the state in countries with the democratic tradition like England and the United States," he tells us, "is not the danger of violent persecution but rather that of the crushing out of religion from modern life by the sheer weight of a state-inspired public opinion and by the mass organization of society on a purely secular basis. Such a state of things has never occurred before because the state has never been powerful enough to control every side of life. It has been a state with limited functions, not a totalitarian state. . . . Today the conflict is a deeper and a wider one. It goes to the very roots of life and affects every aspect of human thought and action." [7]

[7] Dawson, Christopher Henry, *Religion and the Modern State* (1935), p. 57. Sheed and Ward, New York.

That this is not an imaginary danger recent developments in the United States are showing us. In many quarters we find a growing impatience with any expression of opinion, whatever its source, which is critical of the existing social order. This impatience has found expression in the widespread demand that teachers in our colleges and schools shall be required to take an oath of allegiance to the Constitution, a requirement which, however innocuous it may seem on the face of it, may easily be made an instrument of tyranny. It appears in the resentment felt by representatives of the army and navy at any attempt to limit armaments or to oppose the requirement of compulsory military training in government-supported schools. These are indications of a temper which, should the appropriate occasion arise and a plausible leader be found, might be used to limit the freedom of expression which has hitherto been the prerogative of the American citizen.

Were that occasion and that leader to meet there would be no lack of instruments which he could use to enforce his will. The last generation has witnessed a growing extension of the government's activity in the United States until it includes whole areas of life which in the past have been left to other institutions. This is true not only in the sphere of economics and of industry, which have been the primary interest of business, but also in spheres with which the Church has been actively concerned—e.g., education, health, and social welfare. The rise of tax-supported state universities from which the teaching of religion is excluded introduces a problem in the life of the Church whose far-reaching ramifications we are just beginning to realize. So the assumption by the state of responsibility for social security is enlarging the responsibility of government in areas which have hitherto been regarded as the primary concern of the Church. We cannot look therefore at what is going on in Russia and Germany as if it were no concern of ours. It is a warning of what may happen to us here if we are not eternally vigilant.

To sum up in a sentence, what we see in our world is the passing of Christendom, the revival in our time of conditions for which we should have to go back to the third century to find a parallel.

It is against this background that we must approach the questions to which this book is directed. What is the function of the Christian minister in the modern world? The answer can be given in two sentences. It is, first, to see clearly what is the true function of the Christian Church in this confused and troubled world; and, secondly, to fit himself as a minister of that Church to fulfill his part of that task worthily in the place to which God has called him.

It is an answer, I repeat, that can be given in two sentences. But to see clearly what these sentences imply and to live by what we see would be the work of a lifetime.

CHAPTER II

WHAT THE WORLD HAS A RIGHT TO EXPECT OF THE CHURCH

1. How the Roman Catholic Answers This Question

2. How the Protestant Attitude Differs from That of the Roman Catholic

3. Where the Ways Part

4. Some Things Which the World Has No Right to Expect of the Church

5. What the Church Holds in Trust for Mankind

Chapter II

1. HOW THE ROMAN CATHOLIC ANSWERS THIS QUESTION

In the last chapter I raised the question as to the place of the minister in the modern world. We saw that this question has two aspects. First of all we must be clear just what the minister's function is, and secondly, what is the kind of world in which he is to discharge it. That function we saw to be primarily this: to keep men conscious of the fact of God through the practice of public worship. But we saw further that this function must be performed in a world which to a singular degree has lost the consciousness of God and is seeking other substitutes in class or race or state.

The conclusion we reached was that the minister of today has two pressing duties: First, to see clearly what is the function of the Church in the modern world; secondly, to discover how he can perform his part of that function most effectively in the particular locality in which his lot is cast.

Today I invite you to consider with me more fully the first of these duties.

What, then, is the function of the Church in the modern world? Or to put it in a more personal and concrete way, what has the world a right to expect of the Church?

It is important to ask this question because there is no unanimity among Christians as to the answer. The Roman Catholic answers it in one way and we who are Protestants in another. And when we have given our respective answers we find that we differ in the consequences which we draw from them.

It will help to put the Protestant answer to this question in its proper setting if we take a moment at the outset to remind ourselves how our Roman Catholic fellow-Christians answer it. They have a very definite view of the function of the Church in the modern world. That function is, in a word, to give the world an authoritative interpretation of the revelation which God has given to mankind in Jesus Christ and to win men to allegiance to the Roman See, to which as they believe Christ has committed authority as his vicar to mediate his salvation.

This answer is based upon the Roman Catholic understanding of divine revelation, an understanding which has two main aspects: (1) The conviction that Jesus Christ has established in the world an external visible organization to carry on his work, to whose head he has granted the gift of continuing infallibility; (2) that that institution is the Church of Rome.

The history of the Roman Church is the story of the ways through which in season and out of season, by ways direct and indirect, the popes have sought to maintain the

supremacy of the Roman See and to extend it over mankind as a whole.

To be sure, the papacy claims authority only in the realm
of morals and religion. Rome recognizes that there are
duties and responsibilities which belong to the family and
to the state, and these also have divine sanction. But we
have seen how hard it is to draw the line between the
religious and the secular. Rome declares that it is so hard
to draw it that God has committed to his church the responsibility of deciding where and how this is to be done.
Where Rome declares that a moral or religious interest is
involved, even if that interest involves the deposition of a
sovereign or the interdict of a country, loyal Catholics
have no choice but to obey.

In countries with autocratic government there has
seemed nothing inherently unreasonable in the claim made
by the popes to authority of this kind. It was in principle the same kind of authority which the king or emperor claimed for himself. The pope, like the emperor, was
the ruler of a state, with geographical boundaries and independent rights, and it was natural that as such a ruler he
should regulate his relation to other rulers by the methods
usual among the heads of civil states; in other words, either
by treaty or by war. Such treaties, defining the rights and
privileges of the papacy, are known as concordats. The
difference between the position of the popes and other
rulers consisted in the fact that when a dispute arose as to
the respective spheres of church and state the pope as vicar
of Christ, exercising his authority on earth, claimed the
right to decide where that line should be drawn, and when

that right was challenged, to take any measures that might be necessary to enforce his authority.

That right the popes still claim; but in a democratic country like our own, where for more than a century and a half there has been complete separation of church and state, this claim raises perplexing questions. How can the obligation which as American citizens good Catholics owe to the country of which they are citizens be reconciled with the obedience which they owe to the pope? The Roman Church deals with this difficulty in an original way. No doubt, we are told, the relation between church and state in America is from the point of view of the Roman Church far from ideal. But we must judge it not by the ideal but by comparison with other conditions which the Roman Church faces in the world today, say in Russia or Mexico or Germany.

Were America what every good Catholic wishes it might become, a truly Christian country—that is, Christian in the sense in which the Roman Catholic understands Christianity—then all Americans would recognize the propriety of the claim the pope makes and there would be no hardship in its enforcement. In the meanwhile the Church, which has learned by centuries of experience to be all things to all men, realizes that the friendly attitude which the American government takes toward religion gives it opportunities to carry on its propaganda in freedom. This attitude of toleration is far preferable to the attitude of persecution or restraint to which the Church is exposed in many other countries. No doubt there are many limitations upon their freedom of action which Catholics regret. Such a limitation is presented by the public school system. Instead of taxing them for the support of the public schools, from which the formal teaching of religion is excluded, Catholics would like the government to recognize and support their parochial schools as part of the system of national education. Nevertheless the freedom to carry on their religious mission without restraint is so great an advantage that good Americans like Cardinal Gibbons and Governor Smith are quite sincere in saying that they find no conflict between their religion and their citizenship. While for those of us who raise the awkward question what would become of religious freedom for the rest of us if the Catholics should come to complete power, they have the comforting answer that that is so extremely improbable that it would be foolish for us to worry about it.

2. HOW THE PROTESTANT ATTITUDE DIFFERS FROM THAT OF THE ROMAN CATHOLIC

In contrast to this clear-cut and uncompromising doctrine the Protestant finds himself at first sight at a disadvantage. Since he can turn to no single authoritative voice which can speak for Protestantism as a whole, he is obliged to base his formulation of the Protestant view of God's purpose for society upon the utterances, and, still more, upon the practices of many different bodies.[1]

In theory, to be sure, Protestants unite in accepting the Bible as the compendium of the divine revelation, both in matters of faith and of practice, and so the final test by

[1] In this and the following pages I have used some paragraphs from my book, *Church and State in Contemporary America.* Cf. pp. 237-245.

which all conflicting views must be judged. But in fact not all Protestants are agreed as to what the Bible teaches. The consensus of which we are in search must be obtained therefore, if at all, by the democratic process of consultation and experiment. But here we find that the provision for such consultation in Protestantism is very inadequate. Neither in the individual communions nor in their federated and co-operative agencies has any adequate attempt been made to formulate in a systematic manner the principles which should regulate the social activity of the churches and define the nature and limits of their corporate responsibility.

It is not meant by this that no attempt has been made to define the responsibility of the Church on social issues. Many such statements have been made both by individual denominations and by groups of Christians acting collectively. *The Social Ideals of the Churches* [2] is such a statement, and the Declaration adopted by the churches at the outbreak of the World War is another.[3] But it is meant that these statements are for the most part either so general as to give no guidance as to the way in which the ideals held up are to be realized or else are confined to specific situations or to particular aspects of the Church's task. They do not give us a comprehensive statement of the principles which should control the social activity of the non-Roman churches that is comparable either in

[2] New and Revised Edition as Passed by the Quadrennial Meeting of the Federal Council of Churches at Indianapolis, December 8, 1932. (New York, 1933.)

[3] Brown, W. Adams, *The Church in America* (New York, 1922), pp. 97-99.

thoroughness or in regulative influence with the great encyclicals of the popes on social questions.

It is true that when we come to application we find that the agreement between Roman Catholics is less than might have been anticipated. While all Catholics accept the great encyclicals as authoritative, if not in the strict sense infallible, they differ widely as to the practical consequences to be drawn from their acceptance. Interpreters as far apart as Father Coughlin and Cardinal O'Connell alike claim to be loyal exponents of the teaching of the popes. Yet between one or other of these rival exegetes it would seem that each good Catholic is forced to choose for himself.

Protestants, then, have no monopoly of difference on social questions, nor are they alone in owning as supreme authority one which admits of differing interpretation. They differ only in having no single final court to which differences, when they arise, can be referred for final adjudication.

It does not follow, however, because no such court exists that there is no consensus of belief among Protestants, but only that the methods which we take to determine it must be such as are consistent with the Protestant conception of authority. All Protestants agree that the Church has the duty of holding before its members the ideals of human conduct set forth in the Bible and exemplified in the person, life, and teaching of Jesus Christ. They agree further that what that teaching involves for present conduct must be determined by the Christians of each generation in accordance with their understanding of the Biblical teaching, as that teaching is interpreted to them by the Holy Spirit.

Nevertheless, in all the Protestant communions there has grown up a common tradition as to social duty which tends to become the conviction of the group. Even where the doctrine of the individual's direct responsibility to God is held most strongly there is nevertheless an unconscious influence which results from his contact with other members of the Church in common worship, work, and thought. This influence, working simultaneously upon many different individuals, tends to build up a quasi-authoritative opinion which carries great weight with the membership and attains in time a positive quality and color by which we recognize the attitude of the group and its consequences in the field of conduct.

In the study of Church and State already referred to we find the following formulation of the points on which there is widespread, if not universal, agreement among Protestants today:

1. That the gospel has a message for society as well as for the individual.

2. That the Church as the bearer of this message holds a unique place and responsibility among human institutions which it can surrender to no other institution, not excepting the state.

3. That man as we know him today is finite and sinful, and that sin affects every phase of his social as well as of his individual life, including his life in the Church.

4. That the fact of this imperfection does not relieve men from the responsibility of bringing Christian principles to bear upon all phases of life, not only as individuals

but as members of society. Whether as parents, workers, artists, teachers, or citizens, it is their duty, so far as in them lies, to act as Christians should.

5. That among human institutions the state has a position of special importance. Whether we regard it as an original creation of God or as a necessary instrument for mitigating the evil effects of sin, it has a place to fulfill in the providence of God which entitles it to the respect and, under all normal circumstances, to the obedience of the Christian.

6. That it is the responsibility of the state to maintain order in society, to protect its citizens from any attack, whether from without or from within, which threatens their security, and to secure to each of its constituent units —the family, the school, the organizations of agriculture, industry, commerce, and finance—the conditions which make possible the peaceable discharge of their functions. In particular it is its duty to guarantee to the Church the liberty which it requires to discharge its God-given function as witness to the gospel.

7. That it is the duty of the Church to pay to the state the respect which is its due, to obey its laws so far as they are in accordance with the will of God as revealed in the Scripture and in history, and to inculcate upon its members the due discharge of their duties as citizens. Where, however, the state takes action which violates Christian principles, it is the responsibility of the Church to point out its fault, and where it invades the province which is the distinctive prerogative of the Church to resist at all costs.

3. WHERE THE WAYS PART

While most Protestants would accept the above statements as adequate as far as they go, they differ in the interpretation they would give to them and the consequences they would draw from them. Among contemporary American Protestants no less than three different views are held as to the social responsibility of the churches. These views differ so widely as to limit the possibilities of common action.

In the first place, we have the view most definitely represented by the Lutheran churches that the Church, while committed by the gospel to a social witness which is co-extensive with life, is precluded by its constitution from taking part in political activity. This does not mean that the Church has no responsibility for influencing political action, but only that that influence must be indirect, through the training which it gives its members as to their civic responsibility. As a citizen the Christian has the right, and it is his duty, to see that, so far as his influence prevails, Christian principles find social application in political activity.

Such a statement, however, true though it may be as far as it goes, does not accurately measure the difference which separates many Lutherans from their fellow Christians of other communions. That difference appears not simply in their view of the relation of the Church to political activity, but in their view of the significance of that activity in any form. On this point Lutherans are inclined to take a more pessimistic view than their fellow Christians of other communions. Many of them would take the position that the sin of man has so far affected all phases of his social life that it is hopeless to expect any complete reconstruction of society according to Christian principles. It is sufficient to ask of the state that it maintain public order and guarantee public security, and whatever it asks of the citizen in the discharge of this function it is the duty of the citizen to do.

At the opposite extreme we find a group of Christians who not only believe that it is the duty of the Church to bring Christian principles to bear upon all phases of man's social life, including politics, but who are convinced that, in the gospel, Jesus has given us definite instructions how this should be done. Not all these Christians are agreed as to what this instruction is. Some take the pacifist position and make uncompromising opposition to war the supreme Christian duty. Others see in war simply the extreme example of organized selfishness and would commit the Church to advocacy of a radical reconstruction of society along socialist or even communist lines. But they are alike in this, that they identify Christianity with the acceptance of a particular social program for which they invoke the sanction of the Church.

Face to face with this antithesis the majority of American Protestants take an intermediate position. Unlike the extreme Lutherans, they believe that it is the duty of the Church to work for the Christianization of society, and that there is nothing either in the nature of man or the purpose of God which makes this an impossible ideal. On the other hand they are suspicious of any program which offers a short cut to this goal. Even though they recognize that war as carried on by modern states today is wrong, they are not convinced that there may not be conditions when failure to resist wrong by force may not involve a greater evil. All social life, they have come to feel, involves compromise. Even the most radical pacifist pays taxes that help to support the army and navy, and so in fact shares responsibility for the system he condemns. But somewhere there comes a point beyond which compromise may not rightfully go. Here many perplexed spirits feel they have a right to look to the Church for guidance, which up to the present time it has not given them in any adequate way.

It is the purpose of these studies to suggest ways in which this guidance may be given and to point out some of the consequences which follow for the work of the minister.

4. SOME THINGS WHICH THE WORLD HAS NO RIGHT TO EXPECT OF THE CHURCH

It will help us to see our way clearly through the perplexing questions involved in the relation between the Church and the world if we begin by reminding ourselves of some things which the world has no right to expect of the Church.

For one thing the world has no right to expect of the Church *a complete solution of our existing economic and political problems.*

We have seen that some of our fellow Christians are not content to accept this limitation. They believe that the Church should not only hold up before men the type of social ideal for which we ought to strive, but that it should show us in detail how that ideal ought to be realized. I have some English friends who are strong advocates of what is known as the Douglas plan. The Douglas plan, if I understand it, is a particular way of using government credit to solve our present economic and financial difficulties. Whether it is a sound or an unsound plan I do not feel wise enough to know. That will have to be determined by experiment. But these friends of mine are not content to wait for the outcome of the experiment. They wish to commit the Church to the advocacy of that plan here and now. They wish ministers to preach it as the way to the millennium and to mobilize all their resources to get people to accept it.

This is typical of an attitude which has not a few advocates today. They feel so deeply the sorrows and dangers of mankind and they are so convinced that they have themselves discovered the right solution for these evils that they wish to commit the Church as a whole to the advocacy of their particular panacea. The difficulty is that the solutions they offer us do not agree. Some want us to join the League of Nations and to add our powerful aid to the establishment of a system of sanctions, while others feel that uncompromising pacifism is the only proper position for the Church. Some feel that socialism offers the only adequate remedy for our economic ills. But when we ask what particular type of socialism the Church should support, we find that they are not agreed. Some would commit the Church to the Russian brand, others to the more moderate type advocated by Norman Thomas.

Now there are two reasons why the demand which these radicals make upon the Church is an unjustifiable demand. It is unjustifiable in the first place because we who are ministers are not wise enough to know what is the true solution of our economic and political ills. As to the goal we may be clear. On matters of principle we may see eye to eye. But when it comes to application, there are countless questions of detail on which we lack complete information and as to which men equally honest may disagree. It would be fatal to the moral authority of the Church to commit that authority to the advocacy of any panacea, however plausible, which may be discredited by the experience of later generations.

In saying this we have already anticipated the second of the two reasons why the demand thus made upon the Church is unreasonable—namely, that it diverts attention from the primary responsibility of the Church, which is to remind men of the fact of God and to keep constantly before their minds those eternal verities which outlast the changes of the years. Civilizations may come and go; empires may rise and fall; the Church goes on. For it is a witness to those abiding principles which have their seat in the mind and heart of God.

Having said this, however, with all the definiteness and force I can command, let me hasten to add that this does not mean that the world has the right to expect of the Church *a complacent acceptance of things as they are.* There is a view of the relation of the religious and the secular which tries to draw a definite line between the two and to restrict the Church to the religious sphere in such a manner that it has no responsibility for passing judgment on religious grounds upon the evils of our existing social system.

Those who would have us take this position are animated

by very different motives. Some of them are sincerely religious people whose piety is of a mystical type. They believe that a man serves God most acceptably when he withdraws from the world and communes with him from the depths of his own soul. Others frankly resent the Church's criticism of the conduct of their business and find an excuse for this resentment in a narrow view of the responsibility of the Church.

Let me give you two illustrations of this sharp chasm between the religious and the secular, one from the more narrowly intellectual field, the other from that of contemporary business.

During the trial of my colleague, Dr. Briggs, for heresy many years ago one of the prosecutors was a professor of geology in one of our leading universities. When taxed by one of his friends with the apparent inconsistency of his conduct, he gave the following answer: "You ask me how I, a man of science, can attack a theological professor for trying to introduce scientific methods into the study of religion. My answer is very simple. I keep my science and my religion in two compartments with a high wall between. If the wall should break down and my science should get over into my religion, good-by to my religion."

The other example is in the field of business. It is an article by a well-known manufacturer which appeared with editorial approval in an issue of *Nation's Business*,[4] the official organ of the Chamber of Commerce of the United States. In this article, entitled "Render unto Caesar," and described as an open letter to the Administrative

[4] November, 1935.

Committee of the Federal Council of Churches, the whole tendency of the churches to judge modern business by standards of Christian principle was condemned as invading a field which was not properly theirs.

Now I am not here as an apologist for the Federal Council of Churches, and do not presume to say whether in any particular case the criticisms which they may have made upon existing business practices were or were not well taken. What concerns us here is something infinitely more important, the responsibility of the Church to bring Christian principles to bear upon every aspect of our social and political life. We may not know in any particular case what is the cause of the evil from which the world is suffering. We may not see in detail what is the particular remedy that needs to be applied. But as long as anywhere in our social life there is injustice and cruelty, preventable suffering and needless distress; wherever men judge conduct, either their own or that of society at large, solely by standards of financial profit and loss and ignore the human needs and values which may be trampled underfoot in the process; wherever, in short, men act as if they were citizens only of the world of politics or business and forget that they are at least potentially citizens of heaven: there the Church has a responsibility which she neglects at her peril. If precedent were needed, the example of the Old Testament prophets would be justification and to spare.

Once more—and this is a point which is not always so generally recognized—the world has no right to expect of the Church that *its members should themselves completely realize the ideal they hold up.*

I say, should completely realize. I do not say that the world has no right to expect of the Church that its members should take their ideal seriously; that they should show by their conduct as well as by their words that when they talk of the Fatherhood of God and the brotherhood of man they mean what they say. On the contrary it is because so many church members fail to do this that they are subjects of just criticism by men of the world. But I do mean that the world has no right to expect of church members a standard of perfection to which they themselves make no claim and which, save in rare instances, is reached by finite and sinful men only through enlarging experience, earnest prayer, and long-continued discipline.

To be a church member does not mean that one has done once and for all with his limitations and imperfections. It does not mean that he has entered a class which gives him a right to look askance at his fellows who have made no profession of religion as if he were holier than they. But it should mean, and if we take our Christianity seriously it will mean, that he has definitely accepted the Christian ideal as his own, that he has seriously put his hand to the task of making his life over, and that when he calls his fellows in business or politics to accept Christ's standard of helpfulness and service he is asking them to do nothing else than what he is trying to do himself.

And yet how seldom do we find critics of the Church accepting this inevitable limitation. I have read books by travelers who have censured our foreign missionaries because they were people like the rest of us, trying to make their homes bright and pleasant, to give their children the best possible education, and to exercise a modest hospitality when visitors came. I have known missionaries who have denied themselves in order to provide a generous meal for some travelers who had been commended to their care only to be criticized because the meal they had served was as dainty as that to which the visitors were accustomed at home. Indeed I once heard a foreign missionary accused of the heinous crime of owning a piano.

Such examples may be trivial, but they remind us of a widespread misapprehension—namely, that the world has a right to expect of the Church that it succeed in realizing in its members completely and at once the standard it holds up for all. "It is not as a company of the righteous that the Church should bear its witness, but as a company of sinners calling their fellow sinners to repentance." [5] "The Church," to use the striking phrase of a contemporary preacher,[6] "is a society which hazards her reputation by association with the unworthy, and so perpetuates the incarnation of her Lord."

5. WHAT THE CHURCH HOLDS IN TRUST FOR MANKIND

What then has the world a right to expect of the Church? This at least: (1) A unifying and life-giving gospel, (2) an unconquerable faith in its ultimate supremacy.

The first thing that the world has a right to expect of the Church is a unifying and life-giving gospel.

If there is one thing which the experience of the last dozen years has demonstrated beyond the peradventure of a

[5] *Op. cit.*, p. 260.
[6] Buttrick, George A. (in a sermon of April 11, 1937).

doubt, it is that man's supreme need is for a gospel. If we ask what Stalin or Mussolini or Hitler offers the young men whom they are summoning to their standard, the answer can be given in a single word: a gospel. They have a message of hope that lifts men above the dull monotony of a life of routine and offers them something that opens a wide vista and a perennial interest. They ask them to join in remaking their country after the pattern of an ideal. And when they are asked what they have to offer as reward, they answer: the privilege of sacrifice.

And the amazing thing is that they have their response. One can hear much in criticism of what is going on in the different countries that are under dictatorship: the dissatisfaction with the curtailment of freedom, the disappointment at the change of old habits, the restlessness which is due to uncertainty as to the longer future, the sorrow that comes with the parting of old ties. But there is one thing on which the returning visitors are all agreed. These dictators have won the young, and they have won them because they have offered them what the heart of man most of all desires—a gospel.

But alas, to those of us who have learned something of the treasures of the Christian gospel, how pitiful these substitutes seem. They lack the two distinctive features of our Christian gospel: (1) Its theistic basis, (2) its universality. Russia offers us a brotherhood without a Father, Germany a God whose worship is confined within boundaries of nation or race.

If we ask more in detail what the Christian gospel adds to those rival gospels which compete with it today for our allegiance—the gospel of communism, with its exaltation of class; and the gospel of nationalism, with its exaltation of race—three factors stand out above the rest as constituting our distinctive message: the living God, his revelation in the historic Christ, the Church as the society which Christ has founded to be the herald and foretaste of his Kingdom.

First of all the living God. Over against all views that would persuade us that the boundaries of our knowledge stop where science stops, Christianity reminds us of the living God, who alone gives meaning and purpose to nature and who has revealed himself to us through Jesus Christ, not as our Father only, but as the Father of all mankind.

Secondly, the fact that the living God has revealed himself through Christ as the redeemer of mankind. I spoke a moment ago of the Church as a company of sinners. And that is true. But there is a qualifying word which our Christian gospel adds, without which it remains a half-truth. It is a company of sinners who have been redeemed by Jesus Christ. All that that redemption means we cannot stop to unfold here. It is enough to say that it makes possible hope, where else there would be despair, and joy where sorrow had undisputed right of way.

Thirdly, the fact that this redemption is not simply individual, but social. The fellowship into which the gospel invites us is not simply a fellowship with those who are living here and now. It is a communion which has no limits of space or time, but takes in those of every age and name, who through Jesus Christ have discovered their sonship to God and are now conscious of their citizenship in his eternal Kingdom. It is a communion which affects all parts of life—family, and business, and politics alike—and will be satisfied with no goal short of the complete supremacy of Jesus Christ in every relation of life.

The first thing then that the world has a right to expect of the Church is a unifying and life-giving gospel. Having said this we have said in principle all that needs to be said. But what our statement means cannot be completely understood unless we add that, having this gospel, the world has a right to expect of the Church an unconquerable faith in its ultimate supremacy.

When I say that the world has a right to expect of the Church an unconquerable faith in its ultimate supremacy, I am not thinking only or even chiefly of intellectual belief. That that is necessary goes without saying. I am thinking of that more significant conviction which shows itself not in word but in life.

We have had occasion more than once in this chapter to criticize the philosophy of communism. But one truth Marx uttered which we who are not communists may well lay to heart. He said that if you wish to know what a man really believes you must learn what part of his professed creed finds expression in action. We are not saved by our works, but we recognize the faith that saves by the works of which it is the spring.

If you ask me what is the greatest weakness of the Church today, it is not loss of belief in the doctrines of Christianity, though that loss is a fact and should cause us serious concern. It is the failure on the part of those who say they believe to take the implications of their creed seriously. The world, as we have seen, has no right to ask perfection of Christians, but it has a right to expect that they should be in earnest in their effort to realize the type of life to which their faith commits them.

It was commitment such as this that gave birth to modern missions and inspired its pioneers to their heroic achievement. It was commitment such as this which led prophets of the social gospel like Walter Rauschenbusch to broaden their vision until it took in the whole range of human interest. It is commitment such as this that we must still make our own today if we are to meet the rival faiths that are trying to win the world to their gospels. Too long we have been content to wait upon events. It is time that we should be up and doing.

It is heartening to realize that in all branches and sections of the Church there are men and women who realize this fact and who are ready to respond to enlightened leadership when it comes. Everywhere we sense a feeling that a crisis has been reached and that upon what we say and do and think and feel in the days that lie immediately ahead momentous issues depend.

CHAPTER III

THE SCIENTIST'S SUBSTITUTE FOR GOD: NATURE

1. PROPOSED SUBSTITUTES FOR GOD

2. THE SCIENTIST'S REASON FOR STOPPING WITH NATURE

3. THE SCIENTIST'S DIFFICULTY WITH THE THEIST'S GOD

4. HOW THE NEW VIEW OF NATURE HELPS TO MAKE GOD REAL

CHAPTER III

1. PROPOSED SUBSTITUTES FOR GOD

In the last chapter we raised the question of the function of the Church in the modern world and considered certain expectations which are entertained concerning the Church which seemed to us unjustified. We concluded that it is vain for the world to look to the Church for a complete solution of its political and economic problems, but at the same time that it must not expect from the Church a complaisant acceptance of things as they are. We saw further that while the world rightly rebukes Christians for their selfishness and insincerity so far as they are really selfish and insincere, it is not right to expect of church members an instant and complete realization of their own ideal. They, too, like their critics, are imperfect and sinful men and all that can be expected of them is that they should take their ideal seriously and to the extent of their powers work for its realization in themselves and in their world.

But there are some things that the world has a right to expect of the Church, and we listed two such reasonable ex-

pectations. The world has a right to expect of the Church:
(1) A unifying and life-giving gospel; and (2) an unconquerable faith in its ultimate supremacy.

This definition of the function of the Church sets the
minister his task. He is to be a witness to the gospel which
the Church holds in trust for mankind. He is to be a
helper of men in their efforts to realize what the gospel may
mean for their own lives and for the life of society. He is
to hold ceaselessly before his fellows along all sides of their
complex social life the ideal of brotherhood to which the
gospel commits him, and he is never to lose faith in the
practicability of this ideal, however many and apparently
resistless are the forces that oppose it.

And yet he finds himself called to discharge this task in
a world in which its legitimacy is being challenged as never
before. Unbelief, to be sure, is no new thing. In every
age there have been people who have found belief in God
difficult. The new and disturbing fact about the unbelief in our day is that those who have lost their faith in
God do not seem to be troubled by their unbelief. They
are not conscious that in losing God they have lost anything important. Indeed there are many of them who
glory in their loss as if it were a blessing rather than a misfortune. They tell us that the world would be a better
world if people would realize once and for all that there
is no God; that God is at best a superstition born of the
fancies of a prescientific age, at worst a device of selfish and
unscrupulous exploiters to delude men with hopes of a distant heaven while they rob them of their rightful heritage
of the good things of life here.

It is important that we who are to be ministers of the Christian gospel should understand how this has come about. If we are to commend our faith successfully to those who challenge it, we must know why they do so and what they offer us in exchange.

When we ask these critics of our faith why they have been led to break with a conviction which has satisfied so many of the greatest of our kind, they give us reasons of two kinds. They tell us, in the first place, that the method which religious people follow in their quest of God is unscientific. By this they mean that it is based upon a kind of evidence of which science knows nothing, the kind of evidence religion calls faith. Faith, these critics tell us, is only the religious man's name for wishful thinking. Hence the God religious people worship, even though he be good, is not real.

The other reason is just the opposite. It has to do with the character of the God in whom religious people believe. Their God, so we are told, is a being like themselves, yet without any of their limitations, a transcendent personality to whom they turn for help when they ought to be helping themselves or for consolation when they ought to be helping other people. Such a God is not worthy of our worship. Even if he were real, he would not be good.

The first of these objections is urged upon us in the name of science, the second in that of humanity. Each offers us a substitute for God which is said to be better. The scientist's substitute for God is Nature. The reformer's substitute for God is Man.

I propose in this chapter to consider the first of these

substitutes. It is not the most popular, or the most plausible; but it has powerful advocates, and because they come to us in the name of science and appeal to our reason they deserve a respectful hearing. Wherever else the scientist should have his day in court, surely it is in a college dedicated to the pursuit of truth in an atmosphere of freedom.

2. THE SCIENTIST'S REASON FOR STOPPING WITH NATURE

The scientist's substitute for God is Nature. Nature, we are told, can do everything for us that God can do, and better, since Nature includes the sum of all reality so far as it is accessible to science, and hence knowable by man.

What are the reasons which are given us for putting Nature in the place which for so many centuries religion has assigned to God?

One reason which is given us is that the kind of evidence on which religious people base their idea of God is illegitimate, and the resulting conclusion therefore is untrustworthy.

A second is that the God religion offers us is a personal God and hence can have no place in the world of impersonal law with which science makes us acquainted and of which alone it can take cognizance.

The first reason for rejecting God is the insufficiency of the evidence on which belief in him is based. Science, we are told, bases its conclusions on facts which can be tested and verified. Theology, on the other hand, claims to rest its belief upon a special revelation which comes through miracle. But science knows nothing about miracle. Many alleged miraculous events have been shown to have natural causes. Why may not this be true of them all?

Now it may be admitted that the older form of the argument from miracle was open to criticisms of this kind. It is true that many events once deemed miraculous are now seen to be capable of scientific explanation. But we have today a better conception of miracle. Miracle is not thought of by sensible Christians as an event which contradicts the laws of nature, but only as an event which in some compelling way makes man aware of God. There is nothing in the conception of revelation as modern theology conceives it which opens it to criticism as unscientific or superstitious.

The real difficulty lies deeper. It lies in the assumption that the only kind of verification that is possible to us is that which is reached by the methods of the exact sciences, knowledge in other words which includes no subjective element, or, as we might put it in another form, makes no place for judgments of value. This is a view which is widespread, but when closely examined it is found to lead us to a conclusion which would make science itself impossible.

There are two kinds of questions which we may ask: questions which have to do with what things are and how they happen; questions which have to do with why they are and for what purpose they happen.

We may illustrate this difference in the case of any object which excites our curiosity, from an airplane to the universe. What is this thing we call an airplane? Of what materials is it composed? How is it put together? What fuel does it use? How is it regulated? All these are interesting and important questions, and all of them science can answer for us. But there is another group of questions which we may ask about it. How did there come to be an airplane at all? Who invented it, and why did he do so? And now that it is here and we know how to use it, what are we to do with it? When we have learned to fly it, where shall we go, and for what reason? When we start asking questions of this kind we soon come to the place where science alone cannot help us, and we have to rely upon our own personal judgment.

We may ask similar questions about the world as a whole. What elements does it contain? How are these related? Through what steps have they passed? What laws do they obey? How can they be controlled? All these are scientific questions, and we have built up a mass of knowledge that sums up our answers to these questions. But when we have come to the end of our knowledge we have not come to the end of our curiosity. Who made the world? Or did any one make it? What purpose does it serve? Or does it serve any purpose? When we have mastered its laws as science reveals them to us what use shall we make of them? What is the meaning of this life that we are living, and to what destiny are we called? These are the kinds of questions to which religion professes to bring an answer.

We are brought here to a question of perennial interest, that of the relation between science and philosophy. This question has been a subject of discussion between scientists and philosophers ever since science and philosophy began. Professor William James had his own answer, an entertaining and original answer like all his answers. He summed up the difference in this way: Science expresses the sum of the questions which we have already answered. Philosophy is the name that we give to our study of the questions which still remain unanswered.

I have my own way of describing the contrast, which differs from that of Professor James. Science, I suggest, is the name we give to the group of studies that deals with the kind of questions whose answer we can be content to take at second hand. Philosophy is the name we give to the study which deals with the kind of question that each one of us must answer for himself.

You will notice that the last definition brings in the element of value, or in other words the personal or subjective element. This is in fact the dividing line between philosophy and science as it meets us in the person of its greatest representatives.

The introduction of the subjective element into philosophy, or rather the recognition of its inevitability, does not mean that philosophy itself may not be scientific in its method in the sense that it will carry into all that it does the checks of accuracy, comprehensiveness, and impartiality, which are the distinguishing marks of science wherever we find it. But it does mean that it will apply these to those ultimate questions which we cannot help asking, but which, just because they are personal, each of us must answer for himself. In this sense philosophy itself may be called a science, the science of wisdom. It differs from the wisdom of common sense just in its systematic and comprehensive character. We may describe philosophy as organized common sense. Theology, if it be true to itself, will be philosophy of this kind applied to the study of religion. Its subject matter is God—the central object of religious faith—but God considered as a hypothesis whose trustworthiness theology proposes to test and if possible to verify.

There is nothing in this method of approach which is unscientific. It is only to apply to the consideration of philosophical questions a principle the validity of which every scientist must admit—this, namely, that a postulate of some kind is inevitable if experiment is to go on at all. But a postulate is only the scientific name for what religion calls faith. Science itself makes its postulate of the universality of a physical order and the trustworthiness of our knowledge of it. Why then should not religion make its postulate of the universality of a moral and spiritual order and our ability to know it? All that is necessary is that the hypothesis which religion bases upon its postulate should be defined in such a way as to permit the test to be made. The humanists make their pluralistic metaphysics such a hypothesis—in other words, the belief that the only consciousness in the universe is consciousness like our own. But if they do this for their purpose, there is surely nothing scientifically illegitimate in us theists setting up a hypothesis of our own, provided (1) we know what we are doing, (2) have reasons for doing it which we can state, and (3) state them in such a form as to admit of a test at least as definite as the humanist hypothesis admits.

The real difference then between the scientists who reject the theistic hypothesis and the theologians who accept it turns upon the kind of evidence which is relevant to the investigation and the kind of certainty which it is fitted to produce.

We may illustrate this difference in connection with the classical form of Christian apologetics, the form which is technically described as the arguments for the being of God.[1]

It is not necessary for my purpose here to restate these arguments in detail. It is enough to say that they take their departure from observed phenomena in the universe and in man, and reason from them to a cause which is adequate to produce them. From the fact that we are living in a changing world it is argued that there must be some cause adequate to produce the change (the cosmological argument). From the fact that the world lends itself to the realization of our purposes it is inferred that there must be a purposing mind to account for the adaptation (the teleological argument). From the presence of spiritual ideals and values the conclusion is drawn that the cause which has produced them must itself have the qualities of meaning and of value (the ontological and moral arguments). So by a series of considerations analagous to those which we use in other realms the conclusion is reached that there must exist a personal God, in some sense like us, though infinitely greater, who is responsible for this universe in

[1] In this and the following pages I have used some paragraphs from my book, *Pathways to Certainty* (New York, 1930), which sum up the argument for the Christian view of God more concisely than I can put it in any other words. Cf. especially pp 155, 156; 160-162; 166-171; 181-186.

which we live, and with whom therefore we may have direct relations in our daily lives.

And to many minds over many centuries this way of establishing God's existence has appealed as not only religiously satisfying but as scientifically legitimate. Even Kant, the most acute of all the critics of the arguments, admitted that the teleological argument at least made a strong appeal and that it deserved to be treated with respect. Yet he argued that when closely analyzed it involved a fallacy—namely, the surreptitious introduction into the conclusion of a factor not contained in the premise. The professed purpose of the argument is to discover a cause adequate to account for the world we see, but the implied assumption is that this cause must at the same time be such as to satisfy the religious longings and needs of man. But this result is possible only as we read into the evidence data which our religious intuitions supply; in other words, as we introduce into our procedure judgments of value of a kind which ordinary scientific reasoning excludes.

We may admit that so long as we confine ourselves to explanation in the narrower sense, the kind of explanation with which alone the exact sciences are concerned, this criticism is legitimate. But we have seen that there is another kind of question which we may ask than those which science asks and another kind of explanation which is possible than those which it gives. We may ask, not what kind of cause we can demonstrate to be necessary to account for the effects we see, but what kind of cause gives us the most adequate and satisfying *explanation* of these

[72]

effects. When we do this the matter is put in a new light. Here the judgments of value, which reasoning in the narrower sense rules out, become essential, indeed we may say determining factors. When one considers a complicated phenomenon like adaptation it is not simply the brute facts used that are relevant to the conclusion, but the persons who use them, and no explanation that ignores personal valuation of the facts has dealt adequately with all the data.

Interpreted in this broader sense, the old arguments retain a perennial significance. Whether we agree with Kant that in spite of their plausibility the cosmological and teleological arguments involve a fallacy which more rigorous analysis will uncover, or with many theistic writers acknowledge their validity within definite limits, the fact remains that for multitudes of persons the way of approach followed by these arguments is the path which has actually led them to their conviction of the existence of God. Through the experience of dependence and of limitation which is forced upon us by the events of every day we are reminded of the greater forces by which we are encompassed. Contemplating the ceaseless procession of the years, with the changes which they bring with them in night and day, summer and winter, youth and age, life and death, we cannot help wondering who, or what, is responsible for this endless variety. Turning to nature in our need of food and shelter and warmth and light and all the myriad and ever-growing necessities of man, we find her ministering to our uses and it is natural, one might say almost inevitable, that we should conclude that what lends itself to the service of mind must have had mind concerned in its making. Granting that we cannot demonstrate the existence of God in this way, it is still true that multitudes of highly intelligent people have been convinced that of all possible explanations of the world that can be given that of theism is the most reasonable.

When we turn our attention from the outer world to the inner, the evidence of adaptation grows still more impressive. The spiritual world too has its laws, and these laws disclose themselves to the sensitive spirit. These laws too, like the more familiar laws of the physical sciences, have their basis and their illustrations in nature. The moralist's belief in an objective moral order, to which he attributes universal validity, is confirmed not only by the discovery of recurrent elements in the differing moral codes to which the peoples have given their allegiance but by the disastrous consequences which have followed their persistent violation. So the artist's belief in an ideal world of beauty of which he is not simply inventor, but revealer, is confirmed by the existence of common objects which through all fluctuations of taste have maintained their appeal to lovers of the beautiful. How better account for the persistence of these ideals of goodness and beauty than by postulating, with the prophets of theistic religion, a supreme personality who realizes in himself, or is realizing through others, the ideals after which all lesser persons are striving.

3. THE SCIENTIST'S DIFFICULTY WITH THE THEIST'S GOD

But there is a second difficulty which our critics find with the theistic hypothesis, and that is that the kind of

God whom the theist postulates can find no place in the universe as we have come to know it today. Granting that we can establish the fact of God, it is not the kind of God we human beings need. The God of theism is a personal God, not simply in the sense of being himself personality (theologians are the first to recognize that when we speak of God as personal we are speaking in figures), but in the sense in which he is interested in us who are persons and can do for us the things we need to have done.

But the world that modern science has revealed to us is so different from the old world of our fathers that it seems impossible to believe that the kind of God who is appropriate to our modern world can be the kind of God who can do for us what they believed that he could do.

Many different factors have combined to produce this alteration of mood, some of them the result of changes in our view of the physical universe, others of changes in ourselves which are the result of our experience with the universe.

Jesus lived in a world that was limited in space and time. The earth was a flat surface, fixed in space, with the firmament above in which the heavenly bodies revolved, while below was Sheol, the land of the dead, to which the spirits of those who had passed away descended at death. It was a world that had had a definite beginning and would have as definite an end. Indeed as late as the seventeenth century a theologian was found who could date to a year the time of its beginning, even if he was not able as definitely to predict the date when it would end.[2] This world, so limited in space and time, was inhabited by a multitude of spirits, good and evil, who participated in its affairs in various ways. They were the cause of many of the misfortunes from which man suffered, notably insanity and disease. They were also the source of many of his blessings, such as ample crops, recovery from sickness, and victory in war. Protestants, to be sure, unlike their Catholic fellow Christians, no longer thought it right to pray to the good spirits, but they were acutely conscious of the danger to which they were exposed from the evil spirits, as the experience of our New England ancestors at Salem abundantly proves.

What is there in common between this world and the world in which we are living today, a world of spaces all but infinite, in which countless suns move in their orbits at inconceivable speed, while new suns are forming from nebulae that light our heaven with their luminous gases; a world as wonderful in its tiniest components as in its most majestic, each atom a little solar system with its own sun (the nucleus) and its own planets (the electrons)? Where is there room in a world like this, where each event has its appointed place in a system in which everything that happens is bound together by immutable laws, for the direct initiative of deity in miracle and revelation? What more natural than to conclude that the kind of God who would be adequate to account for the world of Jesus and of Calvin is wholly inadequate to account for the world in which we are living today?

[2] Archbishop James Ussher (1581-1656).

Yet it is possible to exaggerate the importance of these changes so far as their practical effects on daily life are concerned. Our *theory* of the universe has changed amazingly, to be sure, changed until our imagination grows dizzy. But it is the same universe as it always was and it is doing for us the same things as it always did. The sun still gives us light and the earth food and the night sleep and the sunrise beauty, and we feel about them in our normal moments just as Abraham felt, and Isaiah, and Jesus. For daily life—all the astronomers in the world to the contrary—the earth is flat and fixed and the sun rises in the East and sets in the West and we set our watches by it. Science has told us some things we did not know about these familiar processes which enable us to use them more effectively and to avoid some of the mistakes which our fathers made. And in addition it has revealed to us a whole set of new worlds of which our fathers knew nothing. But it has not made it any less reasonable to use the old world for the well-tried purposes for which men have always used it. Why may we not find similar continuity in the world of our religious experience?

In a recent collection of essays, dealing with the relation of religion and science, Professor Eddington gives us a graphic picture of the contrast between a physicist's theory of the universe and the practical use which he makes of it:

The learned physicist and the man in the street were standing together on the threshold about to enter a room.
The man in the street moved forward without trouble,

planted his foot on a solid unyielding plank at rest before him, and entered.

The physicist was faced with an intricate problem. To make any movement he must shove against the atmosphere, which presses with a force of fourteen pounds on every square inch of his body. He must land on a plank traveling at twenty miles a second round the sun—a fraction of a second earlier or later the plank would be miles away from the chosen spot. He must do this whilst hanging from a round planet head outward into space, and with a wind of ether blowing at no one knows how many miles a second through every interstice of his body. He reflects too that the plank is not what it appears to be—a continuous support for his weight. The plank is mostly emptiness; very sparsely scattered in that emptiness are myriads of electric charges dashing about at great speeds but occupying at any moment less than a billionth part of the volume which the plank seems to fill continuously. It is like stepping on a swarm of flies. Will he not slip through? No, if he makes the venture, he falls for an instant till an electron hits him and gives a boost up again; he falls again, and is knocked upwards by another electron; and so on. The net result is that he neither slips through the swarm nor is bombarded up to the ceiling, but is kept about steady in this shuttlecock fashion. Or rather, it is not certain but highly probable that he remains steady; and if, unfortunately, he should sink through the floor or hit the ceiling, the occurrence would not be a violation of the laws of nature but a rare coincidence.

By careful calculation of these and other conditions the physicist may reach a solution of the problem of entering a room; and, if he is fortunate enough to avoid mathematical blunders, he will prove satisfactorily that the feat can be accomplished in the manner already adopted by his ignorant companion. Happily even a learned physicist has usually some sense of proportion; and it is probable that for this occasion, he put out of mind scientific truths about astronomical motions, the constitution of planks and the laws of probability, and was content to follow the same crude conception of his task that presented itself to the mind of his unscientific colleague.[3]

Why, Professor Eddington asks, should we not follow the same common-sense method in dealing with the realities of religion? We may explain God differently and yet go to him for the same purposes and get the same results.

4. HOW THE NEW VIEW OF NATURE HELPS TO MAKE GOD REAL

When we approach Nature in this way, we find that there is much in the new knowledge which science has brought which makes it easier and not harder to find God in Nature.

For one thing we have a clearer conception of the unity of the world than our fathers had. They divided the world into two parts, sharply contrasted: nature and the supernatural. Nature was the scene of order and permanence, with uniform laws and unchanging processes. The supernatural was the realm of personality and freedom, where new things came to pass and no one could set bounds to the possible. Science was concerned with nature and worked through reason. Religion had to do with the supernatural and gained its knowledge through revelation.

We see today that no such hard-and-fast line can be drawn. Nature and the supernatural—or to put it in more

[3] Eddington, Arthur S., *Science, Religion, and Reality,* ed. by Needham (New York, 1925), pp. 189, 190. By permission of the Macmillan Company.

familiar and less misleading language, the realm of law and the realm of freedom—are not two independent worlds. Rather are they two contrasted aspects of the one undivided world in which we live, and we cannot do justice to all the facts unless we take them both in.

Admitting this fact, however, it makes all the difference in the world where we place our major emphasis, whether we start from the side of uniformity and explain change by that or from the side of freedom and interpret law by that.

A generation ago the first method was in vogue. Materialism was the dominant philosophy of men of science. Personality was not denied, but it was explained as a complicated combination of elements that could all be reduced to material particles. Freedom was an illusion, our judgments of value were regarded as the negligible by-product of a cosmic process completely explicable without them. This way of explaining the world still lives on in some forms of contemporary behavioristic psychology.

But scientists as a whole have moved beyond this narrow point of view. We see today that if we are to reduce everything to a single principle it is just as easy to start with mind as with matter. From whatever source they may come this is a world which most thinkers will admit contains meanings and values. And if the world be one world, it is difficult to see how meanings and values can have come to pass in us if they were not first present in the universe that produced us.

One of the distinguishing features of much of the scientific writing of our day is the recognition that any comprehensive view of the universe must make a generous use of the concept of value. Indeed a writer as judicious as Whitehead finds value an essential element in the constitution of the universe as a whole, present in the electron as truly as in the mind, though in a different way. "Each occasion," he tells us, "in its character of being a finished creature, is a value of some definite specific sort. Thus a mind must be a route whose various occasions exhibit some community of type of value. And the same must be true of a bit of matter—or an electron." [4]

No doubt it is impossible for us to conceive what kind of a consciousness God can have. But it may fairly be asked what kind of a God would he be whose consciousness it was possible for us to conceive? We are dealing here with something so stupendous and unimaginable that all our words are only symbols that suggest some particular aspect of a reality which in its completeness is beyond our grasp. Is it any easier to conceive of the four-dimensional universe of modern physics than of the infinite consciousness of historic theology? If our inability to picture the one is no reason for doubting its existence, why should a similar inability be any greater reason for doubting the other?

But it is not only in its conception of the unity of the universe that modern science helps us, but also in its conception of its mobility. I know I am entering here on a difficult field for the layman and must tread softly. But this at least we may say with confidence, that whatever else

---

[4] Whitehead, A. N., *Religion in the Making* (1926), p. 109. The Macmillan Company, New York.

may be true of the universe of modern science, it is not a dead universe. We hear people sometimes speaking of dead matter. But if matter be dead, what, it may be asked, can life be? In the atom, as modern physics pictures it, electric particles are moving about with inconceivable rapidity, following orbits so irregular and unpredictable as to lead some schools of physicists to endow them with a power of initiative suspiciously like the freedom we like to claim for persons. One would be foolish indeed to base his faith in a free and personal God upon the changing theories of a science as mobile as the science of physics. At least this can be said, that in our modern world belief in a Creative Spirit who is bringing new things to pass is not harder but easier.

This is indeed the conclusion which is drawn by an evolutionist like Lloyd Morgan. Surveying the steps by which the various forms of life have succeeded one another upon our planet, he finds that the uniformity of the series is broken by the appearance of genuinely new types, types for which apparently we find no adequate preparation in the antecedents which science can discover for us. Comparing the possible ways of accounting for this process of emergent evolution he finds the most reasonable explanation to be that which the theists of all ages have given—namely, the creative activity of a personal God. We cannot indeed *demonstrate* the existence of such a God, but accepting the data as given to us by natural piety he finds this the most reasonable of all possible explanations.

So I come back to the point at which I began, that the

real reason why we find it so hard to find God is that we are not looking in the right place, or perhaps not looking at all.

For what does it mean to believe in God in the simple practical way in which this belief meets us in actual religion, not the religion that men talk about, or lecture about, or write learned books about, but the religion by which they live? It means to have confidence that there is something, or some one, in the universe like us, though infinitely greater and wiser, in touch with our lives and able and willing to help us if we comply with certain conditions; some one with whom we can work, some one to whom we can look up, some one with whom we can commune, some one from whom we may derive strength. That is what belief in God meant to Jesus, and to St. Paul, and to St. Augustine, and to St. Francis, and to Martin Luther, and to John Wesley, and to Cardinal Newman, and to Phillips Brooks. And the one thing we need to know is whether there is anything in the discoveries of modern science that has made it any less possible and reasonable to believe in the existence of such a God than it was before.

There is only one way to tell whether this belief is justified, and that is to put it to the test of life. That is what many of our contemporaries are doing, and they tell us that they have found their belief justified by the event. When they have lived by their faith that God is real he has answered their trust and made them more than conquerors over all their difficulties. In their sickness they have found healing, in their suffering solace, for their sins forgiveness. Even death itself has not brought them defeat, since they have been persuaded that the power that gave them life in the first instance can renew it; and in their hour of greatest loneliness and desolation they have been uplifted by the thought of the great cloud of witnesses by whom they were surrounded, the heroes of faith who in hours as dark as theirs have put their trust in the living God and been unafraid.

How this test is to be made in detail and by what criteria its success is to be judged, we shall consider in a later study.[5]

But before we do this, there is another difficulty which our contemporaries find with the idea of God, and that is that even if it did give us the help religious people say that it does, it does so at the cost of diverting us from more important duties. By concentrating our thought upon our own interests and needs it blinds us to the needs of our fellow men. This gives its driving force to the atheistic propaganda against religion as the opiate of the people. The reason for this attack and the measure of truth which it contains we shall consider in the next chapter.

[5] Chapter V, pp. 123-135.

CHAPTER IV

THE HUMANIST'S SUBSTITUTE FOR GOD: MAN

Chapter IV

1. THE MORAL ARGUMENT AGAINST BELIEF IN GOD

In the last chapter I called attention to a serious issue which has been raised for thoughtful people in our day—namely, the challenge by many of our contemporaries of one of the oldest and most persistent of human convictions, the conviction that there is a God in some true sense like us who has the right to our supreme devotion.

That conviction is challenged on two grounds. It is challenged on intellectual grounds by scientists who tell us that the God whom religion offers us is not real. It is challenged even more directly on moral grounds by reformers who assure us that the God whom religion offers us is not good. In the previous chapter we considered the intellectual argument against belief in God and the substitute by which it is proposed to replace it. Today we are to consider the moral argument against that belief and the substitute the moralist has to offer us. The scientist's substitute, we saw, is Nature. The moralist's substitute is Man.

Some time ago a film was exhibited in the United States which had been prepared by the Soviet Government to interpret to the American people the spirit of the new economic order in Russia. Its theme was the transformation brought about in the life of the peasant by the introduction of modern scientific methods in agriculture. One of the pictures represented a group of peasants who in a time of drought had gathered under the leadership of their priests to pray for rain. In vain they bowed their knees and raised their icons. The heavens remained closed. Then came science, with its tractors and its reforestation, and what appeal to God had failed to accomplish reliance upon man had brought to pass.

This faith in man's power to achieve through science what religion alone was impotent to do for him—namely, the good life for all—is the explanation of the antireligious character of contemporary Russian philosophy. Atheism, to many a young Russian today, is more than negation. It is the removal of an obstacle which had barred the way to progress. It is the opening of a door that leads into a larger life.

From a manifesto of a Russian society under the patronage of the Soviet Government I quote the following appeal for an energetic antitheistic campaign in all countries:

"It is the primary duty of Soviet education to withdraw every child from the influence of religion. To the oncoming generation as our pioneers we confide the great task of the war against religion. . . . It is not enough for our society to confine its activity to the Soviet Union. We must penetrate everywhere and transform ourselves into an international organization. From our position at the heart of the Union we must carry on a systematic campaign for the war of Classes. We are against God and against capital."

We may gain some idea of the extent and energy with which this campaign is being carried on from a report issued by the Research Department of the Universal Christian Council at Geneva. From this report it appears that whereas in 1926 the Godless Movement in Russia numbered some 2,421 groups with 87,033 members, in January, 1933, it had 80,000 groups with 7,000,000 members, of whom 1,500,000 were children. It is true that the most recent reports show that there has been a great falling off in the membership of the movement, some reports putting the present membership of the militant group at less than 2,000,000. But this does not mean that there has been any change in the official attitude toward religion, which continues to be one of uncompromising hostility.

It is in the light of facts like these that we must understand the clause in the recently promulgated draft of the new Constitution for Russia in which freedom of religious worship is guaranteed. The same paragraph distinctly specifies as of equal importance the right to carry on propaganda against religious belief, and the government leaves us in no doubt on which side its sympathy lies.

To understand the causes which have produced so extraordinary a situation in a country where for many hundred years Christianity has been the official religion we must remember that the Church in Czarist Russia was a department of the state and was associated in the minds of the revolutionists with the repressive measures which kept the mass of the people in poverty, ignorance, and superstition. Those who preach atheism as good news know nothing of the uplift and inspiration which faith in God has brought to us to whom his worship has supplied the chief motive for service to man.

But the case against much conventional religion can be put in even stronger terms. It is not simply that belief in God has made acquiescence in things as they are easier. It has put needless obstacles in the way of those who are trying to change it. By making God the champion of the *status quo* it has opposed the august sanctions of revelation to man's legitimate protest against preventable wrongs. In the path of every great reform which has won freedom for an oppressed humanity some representative of organized religion has erected his "Thou shalt not" until God, instead of being the symbol of humanity's highest aspirations, has become the most powerful single obstacle to their realization. Humanism, we are told, delivers us from this impossible contradiction. In abolishing God it clears the way for human progress.[1]

You cannot understand the contemporary wave of disbelief unless you take account of this note of moral protest. "You Christians tell us," the humanist says, "that religion ought to make us brotherly, but you yourselves are often selfish. You tell us that it ought to give us courage, but you are afraid to look facts in the face. You tell us that it ought to make us happy, but you yourselves are

[1] Cf. Brown, W. Adams, *Pathways to Certainty* (New York, 1930), p. 18.

worried and anxious. In a word, you tell us that religion ought to make men different from their neighbors, but in fact you are just like the rest of us, only you use pious words and we do not. Well, we are tired of this kind of hypocrisy. If we are to have a religion at all, at least let it be an honest one that deals with facts as they are." [2]

2. SELF-EXPRESSION AS A HUMANIST SUBSTITUTE FOR GOD

What then does the humanist offer us as a working substitute for the faith he would have us discard? The name itself gives us our answer. Since God is ruled out as the object of man's supreme devotion, it is man, he tells us, with whom we must be content. For man is the highest object in nature, the only being who, face to face with evil, refuses to accept it as ultimate and rises against it in protest. It is in man, and man alone, that the humanist finds those ideals and values operative which religion in its dream of an impossible perfection has transferred to God. Christianity itself furnishes the most convincing argument for the humanist case. When Christians would take their belief in the good God earnestly, they have been obliged to turn away from nature, with its vastness and unresponsiveness, and to find their ideal incarnate in the person of a man like ourselves to whom they could say not only "Master," but "brother."

Man, then, not indeed as we see him today, in his selfishness and imperfection, but man at his highest and best,

[3] Brown, W. Adams, "Humanism: What It Is and How to Meet It," in *Humanism: Another Battle Line*, ed. by William P. King (Nashville, 1931), p. 242.

the humanist tells us, is a sufficient object for man's devotion. In the service of man he may find satisfaction for all the longings which in the past have made him turn to religion.

When we ask more in detail what form this devotion to man should take we find two possibilities open to us. Either we may see in the self-development of the individual the chief end of man or we may make the social welfare our supreme endeavor. Some humanists put the emphasis on the first alternative, others on the second. Some offer us self-realization as a substitute for God, others the good of society.

If I had been writing ten years ago on the humanist substitute for God, I should have found it necessary to devote my chief attention to the first of the two alternatives which humanism offers us, that of individual self-expression. If we had put to a humanist of that day the familiar question of the Westminster Confession of Faith, "What is the chief end of man?" he would have answered: It is man's chief end to develop himself and to enjoy himself as much and as long as he can.

The dominant note in the ethics of that day was the autonomy of the individual. The magazines were full of complaints of the narrowness of our conventional standards and learned professors wrote lengthy tomes to explain how ill-adapted to an industrial age were the sanctions which were appropriate in a simpler and more stabilized society. Young people were encouraged by their elders to experiment with delicate matters like sex and religion, and the question whether family or church was to find a place in the society of the future was regarded as at least a proper subject for discussion. The one thing on which there seemed to be general agreement was that any restraint which inhibited individual liberty was an evil from which as far as possible we ought to seek to free ourselves.

Nowhere was this emphasis upon self-expression carried to greater lengths than in education. Instead of a fixed curriculum with definite requirements, the likes and dislikes of the student were allowed to determine his choice of studies. Under the name of the elective system this glorification of liberty was carried to such lengths that the president of a great university, in a recent discussion of contemporary education, has described the situation in which the student in quest of wisdom now finds himself when he passes the doors of a modern American university as "educational chaos."

There are, however, certain very obvious difficulties with the philosophy of self-expression. One is that the attempt of one individual to express himself in one way may bring him into conflict with the desire of other people to express themselves in other ways. Another, and even more serious, difficulty is that the desire of each individual is changing. One does not wish the same things when he is a grown man that he did when he was a child of ten. An ethics that would be truly scientific, therefore, must take full account of this fact of change.

But the difficulty with the philosophy of self-expression as a substitute for God goes deeper. It is the fact that there is no such thing as an isolated individual. Man realizes himself only through relation to other persons or to that system of collective relationships that we personify under such terms as "family," "class," or "nation." It is not when he stands most alone that the normal man feels most himself, but when he is associated with his fellows in some cause which calls forth his active goodwill.

3. DEVOTION TO THE COMMON GOOD AS A SECOND SUBSTITUTE

This reference to active goodwill forms a natural transition to the second substitute presented to us by our contemporary humanists—devotion to the social good. This is an end which makes appeal to nobler motives than any which are purely individual. It presents man with an object greater and worthier than self, an object that outlasts not the individual only but all contemporary existence and in its duration and range approximates the eternity which the older theology attributed to the Creator. For man as an individual it would substitute humanity as the true object of man's devotion, not the humanity of today with its imperfections and foibles, but the perfected humanity of the future, when through the appropriation of the new knowledge which science will one day put at his disposal man shall have come to his own.

We may let Professor Otto be spokesman for humanists of this type. Answering the objection that loss of faith in God condemns man to cosmic loneliness, he suggests that the relinquishment of a companion behind nature may give added value to human fellowship. Let us accept, if we must, "the stern condition of being psychically alone in all the reach of space and time, that we may then, with new zest, enter the warm valley of earthly existence—warm with human impulse, aspiration, and affection, warm with the unconquerable thing called life; turn from the recognition of our cosmic isolation to a new sense of human togetherness, and so discover in a growing human solidarity, in a progressively ennobled humanity, in an increasing joy in living, the goal we have all along blindly sought, and build on earth the fair city we have looked for in a compensatory world beyond." [3]

When we ask how this ideal society is to be reached, we find the ways parting. Some humanists believe that the way to realize man's social possibilities is to trust him from the first and to put on him all the responsibility he is able to bear. Others believe that the present generation must be trained for responsibility through a preliminary period of subjection to authority. These divergent views work out in sharply contrasted programs of present-day activity.

Those who take the first view are inclined to be conservative in their attitude toward existing social institutions. They realize that in our approach to a distant goal we must pass through many intermediate steps and be ready to work with those who differ from us in some things for the ends in which we both agree. That is the attitude of a man like Bernard Shaw, who is a Socialist indeed, but who believes that the Socialist Utopia will be realized step by step as little by little the control of the means of pro-

[3] Otto, M. C., *Things and Ideals* (1924), p. 290. Henry Holt and Company, New York.

duction is transferred from individuals or groups to society as a whole.

This conservative attitude appears in the view which many humanists take of the Church. Much as they disapprove of the theology of the existing churches, they recognize that in our complex society there is room for an institution that will do for the society of the future what the Church of today attempts to do, however unsuccessfully, for the society of today. We need an institution to remind us of the ideal we have not yet attained, to furnish us with symbols that express this ideal in ways to affect our emotion, to provide a point of contact for those who accept that ideal as their own, and to be the rallying point for all movements which seek to bring its realization nearer. If the existing churches can be refashioned so as to fulfill this function, they should be conserved. If not, we must create new institutions to take their place.[4]

Some who claim the name of humanist are willing to go even farther in their approach to the traditional faith. Much as they dissent from the meaning which many theists attribute to the word "God" today, they recognize that it stands for values which mankind will not willingly let go. They are willing, therefore, to go on using the term provided they can redefine it in their own way. God, they tell us, is the name we give to our consciousness of the highest social values. It expresses the spirit of the group as it comes to consciousness in the men and women who compose it. For men in general it takes the place that Uncle Sam does for Americans or Alma Mater for college grad-

[4] Sellars, R. W., *Religion Coming of Age* (New York, 1928), pp. 286-288

uates. It is in this sense that Professor Ames calls himself a theist. The God he worships is finite as we are finite, growing as we are growing, and the way to find him is to be our own true selves as we co-operate with our fellows in meeting the ever-changing situations with which our ever-changing life confronts us.[5]

But the way of reconstruction is not the only way open to the humanist. A more direct way is open to him—the way of revolution. Those who follow this path will tolerate no compromise with existing religion. Any attempt to remodel old institutions or to redefine old terms, they tell us, is certain to call up old associations which will lead to false hopes and wrong conduct. When dealing with an error so deep-seated and long-continued as belief in God the only safety lies in a complete break.

The most consistent example of this radical humanism is the communism of contemporary Russia. The Communist is a humanist who, because of his desire to realize the ideal life for man, has adopted atheism as his creed. But to him resignation, far from being the last word of wisdom, is the coward's excuse for evading man's supreme duty. That duty is revolution, individual and social—revolution against a type of religion which either supinely accepts evils as willed by God or makes that will an excuse

[5] It is an interesting question whether this statement exhausts the meaning which Professor Ames puts into the word "God." There are passages in his writings which lend themselves to this interpretation (e.g., *Psychology of Religious Experience*, Boston, 1919, p. 313). There are others, especially in his later writings (e.g., *Religion*, Chicago, 1929, pp. 149-162), which seem to go beyond it. So far as the latter alternative correctly represents Professor Ames' true position, he has ceased to be a humanist in the sense in which we are using the term here and become a theist.

for perpetuating them when they could be prevented. As a good humanist he welcomes the powers that modern science puts into his hands and accepts the obligation to make right use of them. But the end which commands his loyalty and excites his enthusiasm is not the individual's development of his own capacity for self-expression, but the subordination of all his powers to the Communist State. For the achievement of this goal he is willing to make and to ask any sacrifice, even that of life itself. In its name he is prepared himself to give and to demand of others a submission as complete as that required by the older orthodoxy.

It is the view taken of the state which differentiates the Communist philosophy from that of contemporary Nationalism in its fascist form. Both alike magnify the state as having the right to the loyalty and devotion of all its citizens. But to the Fascist, whether he be Italian or National-Socialist, loyalty to the state is justified as inherently excellent, the normal expression of man's highest aspiration, whereas to the Communist this devotion is regarded as a temporary expedient, necessary to be sure, because of the fact of the class war, but at its best only a stage through which the Communist movement must pass on to its ultimate goal, the universal rule of the proletariat in a world from which all classes have disappeared. When that happy time comes there will be no need of force, since all men will do voluntarily what is right. There will be no state, since each citizen will play his part in turn in the exercise of government. There will be no greed, since under the improved system of production and distribution made possible by modern science "each person will take from the common storehouse what articles he needs and as many of them as he needs, and depart. No one will have an interest in buying the surplus, because every one can have what he wants and when he wants it." [6] Reading the picture painted by these missionaries of the social revolution of the happiness and prosperity which awaits those who live to see the coming of the Communist State one is reminded of the prophecies in which the early Christians found solace in their days of persecution with dreams of the good time coming when Jesus would return to earth to establish his Kingdom. We can understand the enthusiasm which is shared by those who really believe, as the early Christians believed, that such a revolutionary change can happen to the world in our own day.

I have chosen Russia as an example of the most radical form of contemporary humanism because it is most prominently in the public eye. But it is only the most striking example of a tendency which is present in other countries and which may be all the more dangerous when it is not clearly perceived. We have seen that even in democratic countries influences are at work which if allowed to go unchallenged would confine freedom within ever narrower bounds and make of the state, which is the agent through which the dominant group expresses its will, an authority which may rightfully claim the uncompromising devotion of all its citizens.

[6] Bucharin, N., and Preobraschensky, E., *A B C of Communism*, Lyceum-Literature Department Workers Party of America, N. Y., 1921, p. 58.

4. WHAT CHRISTIANS HAVE IN COMMON WITH HUMANISTS

So much by way of description. Now what ought to be our attitude toward humanism? With what spirit should we meet its challenge? I believe that we should meet it with open-mindedness and sympathy, recognizing that it could not have attained its present proportions except as a protest against evils for which we ourselves are partly to blame.

What shall we say of a man like Professor Otto who has lost out of his life the kind of a God in whom you and I believe and who yet says, "Nevertheless, I am going to go right on working for my fellowman just as before, even if I can no longer count on God for help"? I think that such a man shows exceptional courage. When I think what faith in God may mean for human life, what it has meant for many of those who are here, the courage it gives, the comfort it brings, the inspiration it affords, the sense of balance and proportion and uplift that it contributes to life, and realize what the man without this faith has lost out of his life, I cannot but admire him as he makes his attempt to carry on without God. I only hope that his courage will last.

But we can go further than this. We can find elements in humanism which we must ourselves appropriate if we are to do justice to our Christian faith. There are three great convictions for which humanism stands, convictions which Christians can share. The first is the conviction of the value of man as man, every last individual of us, wherever and whoever he be. Now that is an essential

Christian truth. Jesus Christ was in this sense the first of the humanists and the greatest. No one had a keener eye for the possibilities latent in the humblest and most despised of his fellows than Jesus. No one took the duty of forgiveness when wrong had been done more seriously or gave more convincing illustration of its revolutionary effects. It was the chief charge against him that he found his friends among publicans and sinners and chose for his disciples simple laymen without knowledge of the law. It is, indeed, the contrast between Jesus' ideal for man and what many Christians have made of that ideal that helps to account for the rise of humanism. When the Russian Communists preach their doctrine of the dictatorship of the proletariat they are giving an exaggerated and one-sided rendering to one aspect of Jesus' gospel, his promise of salvation for the poor.

The second thing that the humanists emphasize is the competency of man, his ability to become what he ought to be. And here, too, they are reminding us of a truth that belongs to us as part of our Christian heritage. For, mind you, the humanist does not say a man can do what he ought alone; he says man can do it when he uses the laws of nature. And to those of us who believe that the laws of nature are the laws of God, the humanist's affirmation of the competency of man is the reaffirmation of an essential truth.

It was not a humanist but a theist who said to some of his neighbors, "Work out your own salvation." It was not a humanist but a theist who said, "I can do all things." But there is a condition on which success depends. And here the ways part. "Work out your own salvation," says the humanist, "for it is Nature through which you work." "Work out your own salvation," says the theist, "for he who worketh in you is God."

The third humanist affirmation is that men are responsible for making use of their power to change this world into a different kind of a world and a better world. And when you ask the humanist in his quiet hours what kind of a world he wants—I say in his quiet hours, not when he is listening to an orator like Hitler or Mussolini—you find it is just the kind of world you and I want, a world of freedom, of brotherhood, and of happiness. But he goes on to tell us that Christians often make religion an excuse for evading responsibility, and if we are honest we shall have to admit that this has too often been true. Where it is true, the thing for us to do is to confess our fault and see to it that we do not offend again.

Even those forms of humanism which seem to us most offensive and dangerous, such as pagan Nationalism and atheistic Communism, retain their hold upon the young on whom they rely for success by their appeal to motives which we cannot but admire. In a world where we find multitudes who expect some one else to support them and whose only question to the state is, What have you to give? we find them saying to their young people, What I offer you is not ease, but sacrifice. Look upon your life as a trust which is given you to be used for an end greater than yourself. You are Germans, or Russians, or Italians, and whatever your country asks of you, you must be proud to give.

[102]

Let no one deceive himself as to what is happening in the world today, as though pride and selfishness alone could explain the rise and extraordinary vitality of these new religions, Communism, Fascism, National Socialism. Selfishness and pride there are no doubt, and to spare, on the part of leaders and of led; motives that are base and that will not bear the light. This always happens when men band themselves together for causes that involve conflict of interests. But selfishness alone will not explain the passionate devotion which is rallying the young men of Russia to the standard of Stalin, the young men of Italy to the call of Mussolini, the young men of Germany to the summons of Hitler. Something larger and nobler is involved, something that appeals to loyalty and justifies sacrifice. These young men have found a larger life, of which their little life is part and in which it finds its true self. What these dictators are offering their followers is a faith that outlasts the present and makes life itself a gift to be gladly, yes even proudly, given. They do not ask these young recruits what they would like to do. They tell them what they must do. And this "must" they bring to them in definite and easily recognizable form, as the demand of a nation or of a party that asks uncompromising commitment to a cause which has the right to demand one's all.

To those of us who have lived through the War it ought not to be necessary to explain the force of this appeal. We have seen it ourselves in those momentous days of 1917, when at the call of our President the colleges of this country were literally emptied of their young men as they rallied to the colors. It was not their desire for gain or their lust for blood which led them to volunteer. It was the conviction that their country needed them, and what their country needed they would gladly give.

And in this connection may I make my protest against those who in the light of our clearer knowledge of the consequences which have followed the Great War impugn the motives of those who entered it. No one who lived through those early days and had firsthand knowledge of the factors which were at work will question the sincerity and unselfishness which led multitudes in every walk of life—and I am not speaking of soldiers only, but of ministers and teachers and men of business—to abandon their ordinary occupations and to offer themselves to their country, to be used in any way and in any place where the nation's need might call.

It is this spirit which the world still needs today, the spirit that is willing to give all for an end that is greater than self. If only the cause for which it were asked were nobler! An English statesman, Lord Lothian, speaking of the new cult of national sovereignty which has turned Europe into a group of warring camps, has called it "demonic." It is demonic because it appeals to the noblest motives on behalf of a course of conduct which is not only destructive of the enemy against whom one fights, but will in the end if persisted in spell self-destruction.

There is nothing, Lord Lothian reminds us, in the claim which the state makes upon the individual which is necessarily evil. On the contrary it is the condition of all ordered and stable social life. It is true that the state makes use of violence, indeed that it could not exist without it. "A great number of the laws it enacts and the changes which it brings about are inevitably objected to by individuals or sections of the community. Yet if the state did not enforce the law, and do so irresistibly, individuals and groups would inevitably begin to use violence or fraud to defend or promote their own rights or interests, and society itself would dissolve in anarchy." [7]

But a power which may be beneficent when used within a definite geographical area for the maintenance of order and the promotion of social justice may have disastrous consequences when applied on a world-wide scale and without the checks which a commonly accepted system of international law supplies.

This is the situation which we face in the world today. Within the individual nation the sovereignty of the state is the only assured defense against anarchy. In the world of nations the assertion of unrestricted national sovereignty threatens mankind with anarchy on a scale unexampled in human history.

Against such a misguided loyalty there is only one defense, and that is a higher loyalty; loyalty to the God who is Lord of nature as well as of individuals and who has made of one blood all the members of the human race. And the one society which in this distracted and war-harassed world exists to remind men of this fact and to summon them to this highest allegiance is the Christian Church.

In an address delivered at Princeton some time ago,

[7] *Religion in Life*, Winter Number, 1937, p. 19.

Professor Einstein, one of the most distinguished of the scholars expelled from modern Germany on account of his race, expressed his surprise that when all other elements of the community had surrendered to the demand of the state for unquestioning obedience—the press, the university, the labor unions, the political parties—it was the Church alone that dared to make its protest.

The explanation of this mystery was given me by a friend who is intimately acquainted with post-war conditions in Germany. It was no sudden awakening of a sleeping church, he tells me, which explains the protest, but only the culmination of a process of rediscovery which had been going on for many years. In the sorrow and tragedy of post-war Germany many a humble spirit, in the pastor's study and in the professor's chair, had been rediscovering God. So when Hitler came to the Church with his demands for unquestioning obedience, they had their answer ready. You offer us a master. You have come too late. We have already found our Master, even the God and Father of our Lord and Saviour Jesus Christ. And from that allegiance no power in heaven or on earth can swerve us.

CHAPTER V

THE MINISTER AS PRIEST: HOW TO MAKE
GOD REAL

1. THE MINISTER AS MEDIATOR BETWEEN GOD AND MAN

2. THE LOSS OF THE GOD-CONSCIOUSNESS IN CONTEM-
   PORARY RELIGION

3. WHAT IT MEANS TO HAVE A GOD WHO IS REAL

4. WHY SOME PEOPLE FIND IT HARD TO REALIZE THE
   FACT OF GOD

5. WHERE GOD MAKES HIS PRESENCE EVIDENT TODAY

6. WHAT TO DO WITH WHAT WE FIND

Chapter V

1. THE MINISTER AS MEDIATOR BETWEEN GOD AND MAN

THUS far we have been considering the world in which the minister must do his work and have tried to discover what is the distinctive contribution which the Church has to make to its tasks and problems. That contribution we saw to be twofold: a unifying and life-giving gospel and an unconquerable faith in its ultimate supremacy.

The Church, to be sure, is not the only institution which comes to men with a gospel. Indeed the pathos and tragedy of the world in which we live consists in no small measure in the fact that it is the scene of the strife of rival gospels. If the minister is to bear his part worthily in this strife, he must see clearly what is distinctive in the Christian gospel and how it bears upon the lives of men in the specific place in which his lot is cast.

In saying this we have answered in principle the question which every thoughtful minister must often have asked himself: What is my special function in this crowded world? It is to help to make God real to a generation that has largely forgotten his presence. Whatever else I may do or leave undone, there is one thing I can do: there is one thing I must do. I must be a witness, a bringer of the good news that God is at work in his world and therefore that we need not fear. And this not by word only, but by life. I must not only talk to men about God. I must help them to realize his presence. In other words, I must be not only a preacher, but a priest.

I know that the word "priest" has an unfortunate ring in Protestant ears. It smacks of sacerdotalism and magic. It seems to suggest that God has endowed the minister with certain supernatural powers denied to his fellows, by virtue of which he can mediate or withhold from them grace not accessible in other ways.

There have been times in the history of the Church when priesthood has meant just this. There are individuals and schools in the Church today who accept, and with conviction, a view of the ministry which draws a sharp line of distinction between priest and people and denies to the latter the mediatorial function which is affirmed of the former.

Against this conception our Protestant fathers protested; but they did this not by rejecting the priestly function of the ministry, but by extending it to all believers. All Christians at heart ought to be priests—that is, persons who help to bring about contact between God and man. For this and nothing else is what priesthood means, in its simplest and most universal connotation. A priest is a mediator, not in the sense that he does for you and me what we cannot do for ourselves, but in the sense that he helps us to bring about a contact with God which will make it possible for us, once that contact is established, to do ourselves, by God's grace, what it is God's will and purpose that we should do.

This point of contact is provided in the most familiar and easily accessible way by the institution of public worship. When we worship, in spirit I mean, not simply in word, we lift our hearts to God in adoration and praise, and we receive from him the motive to repentance and consecration. The priestly office of the minister consists in the fact that his stated contact with his people in the services of the Church gives him this unique opportunity to make more real to their consciousness the fact of God.

2. THE LOSS OF THE GOD-CONSCIOUSNESS IN CONTEMPORARY RELIGION

It is the minister's primary function, I repeat, "to make more real to his people's consciousness the fact of God." I do not say to make it easier for them to *believe* in God. That is important, no doubt, and a great many people are working at this in helpful and effective ways. But it is not this that I have primarily in mind. There is all the difference in the world between believing in God and realizing him. There are a great many people who believe in God quite sincerely but who have no vivid consciousness of his presence. They never think of taking him into account when they plan their day's work. So far as they are concerned, he might as well not exist.

It is not of such purely intellectual belief that I am thinking here—the belief that is expressed in formal creeds and is defined in learned treatises, useful and important as these may be. I am thinking of the practical faith that expresses itself in such homely matters as daily prayer, personal commitment, and the missionary spirit; the faith of men who do what they do because they are sure that it is the will of God, and in this assurance find inspiration and peace—in a word, the faith of people who take God seriously in the simple commonsense meaning that religious people have always given to the word "God."

There are many people in our day—and not a few, more's the pity, in our Protestant churches—who do not believe that such a God-consciousness is possible, and many more who do not believe that it is important, even if it were possible. They do not call themselves Humanists, but they act and feel toward God much as the Humanists do. They do not deny him with their lips. Indeed many of them would be very much offended if you suggested that they did not believe in him. But he plays no appreciable part in their lives. They do not realize him as a continuing presence with whom they have daily contact, as they do with nature or with other persons. He is no longer—in some cases he has never been—a central factor in their consciousness. If you ask them why they go to church, they will give you a variety of reasons: that they like the minister, that they enjoy the music, that they believe in supporting the institution, that it sets a good example to the children—good humanist reasons, all of them. It would never occur to them to say that they go to church because it helps them to realize more vividly the presence of God.

This humanist attitude toward religion has been brought vividly before us in a book which I understand has become one of the best sellers, *The Return to Religion*,[1] by a psychologist named Henry C. Link. The reason which he gives for attending church and advising others to do so is that going to church makes one do every week things that one would rather leave undone. "I go to church," he says, "because I would rather lie in bed late on Sunday mornings, the only chance for a good sleep I have during the week. I go because I would rather read the Sunday papers. I go because I know it will please my old father, when he learns of it, and my parents-in-law whom I shall undoubtedly see there. I go because I meet and shall have to shake hands with many people, many of whom do not interest me in the least. . . . I go, in short, because I hate to go and because I know that it will do me good."[2]

Now we may admit that it is better to go to church for the reasons Professor Link gives than not to go at all; but you will agree with me, I am sure, that this whole group of motives—all of them self-centered rather than God-centered—move in a very different world of thought from that sense of a constraint which could not be evaded which made faith in God so central a factor in the life of the devout souls of an older generation.

One effect of this loss of a vivid sense of the reality of God among church members is a waning of interest in the missionary work of the Church. I do not mean that missions are no longer supported, but that they are not sup-

[1] The Macmillan Company, New York, 1936.
[2] *Op. cit.*, p. 19.

ported with enthusiasm, not at least with the kind of enthusiasm that swept the older generation of college students into the Student Volunteer Movement, or, to take a more recent illustration, that the young men of this country showed when at the appeal of President Wilson they entered the World War. Missions still maintains its place in American Protestantism as a legitimate interest; but it is one among others. It is no longer the supreme interest. It fails to command passionate devotion.

Such at least is the impression which our American Protestantism is making upon thoughtful visitors from the other side. Recently I heard one of the secretaries of the Student Movement, an exceptionally intelligent young Lutheran, describe the impression produced by our American Christianity among the young people he meets on the Continent of Europe. What they miss, he tells us, is the note of passion, the sense of a mission not to be evaded, a "woe is me if I preach not the gospel." To catch this note, he tells us, you have to turn to the secular religions of our day: Fascism with its gospel of nationalism, Communism with its promise of world revolution. Only in Catholicism, both in its Roman and its Anglican forms, does he catch the note of a dominating and overmastering enthusiasm in Christianity.

3. WHAT IT MEANS TO HAVE A GOD WHO IS REAL

You will not think that I exaggerate then when I say that of all the functions of the minister's work this of priesthood is the most important. He is to help men to realize what it means to have a real God and to draw the consequences which follow for life from the discovery.

What then does it mean, I do not say to believe that there is a God, but to have a God who is felt to be real? It means to be persuaded that at the heart of the universe there is a reality in some true sense akin to us, though infinitely greater and worthier, in whom we find the answer to our ultimate questions, the object of our supreme devotion, and in fellowship with whom we may find unfailing inspiration and enduring joy.

Let us analyze this definition to see what it contains. The first thing that strikes us is the word "reality." Whatever else may be true of God he must be real, as real as the table at which I sit or the friend to whom I speak. God is not something I create, but something I find; not something I invent, but something I discover. That is the uniform testimony of the people to whom God has been more than a theory or an idea.

The second thing about God is that he is different. He differs from the other realities of which the world is full, as the whole differs from the part, the cause from the effect, the ideal from its imperfect manifestation. Whatever else God may be, he is the *ultimate* reality, the basic fact in our world of facts, the final authority to whom allegiance is due.

This explains the element of mystery in God. What is like us we can understand, but what is unfamiliar surprises us. And the characteristic emotion which God arouses in his worshipers is surprise. In every age men have thought of God as the august, the wonderful, the awe-inspiring. In God they have found something that transcends their utmost powers either of thought or of action.

Yet with all his strangeness there is something about God that man has felt to be akin to himself. The words he has used to describe God have been words taken from his own experience, the highest and the best he could find: Lord, Master, King, Father, Friend. That is the wonderful thing about God, that he is the paradox of paradoxes, at once like us and unlike, at once familiar companion and transcendent Lord.

One thing more must be added to make our analysis complete. However God is conceived and wherever he is found he is always one with whom the worshiper stands in personal relation. He is not the object of distant reverence merely. He is the recipient of personal devotion and loyalty. Religion, said a great Dutch philosopher many years ago, begins when a man applies the personal pronoun to God. God is one to whom one says "Thou." In the words of Augustine: "Thou hast formed us for Thyself, and the heart of man is restless until it finds its rest in Thee."

This personal relationship may find expression in all phases of our experience. God is one in whom we find the answer to our ultimate questions. He is one who furnishes us with a supreme object for our devotion. He is one who offers us the satisfying fellowship.

When I say that we find in God the answer to our ultimate questions I do not mean that faith in God relieves us of the responsibility of the patient investigation through which modern science has won its amazing triumphs. I do not mean that faith gives us a short cut to certainty which relieves us of individual responsibility for decision. But I do mean that when we have come to the utmost reach of the knowledge that science makes possible and face the encompassing mystery we are not left a prey to helplessness and despair, but may carry with us along life's uncharted way the assurance that, though we cannot see clearly, there is one who does. I mean that when we have done our best to reach a wise decision and find ourselves still in the dark, we may find solace in the conviction that, though we may decide wrongly, there is one who will decide aright; and in trust of him and loyal obedience to his will, so far as he gives us to see it, we may find our peace.

Again, when I say that in God we may find the supreme object of our devotion I do not mean that in order to be true to God's service we must turn our back upon the lesser loyalties of family, of business, of nation, of race, of class. I do not mean that we must enter a monastery and leave to the politicians and the statesmen the task of bringing order and decency into our confused and struggling world. But I do mean that, however sincere may be our devotion to nation or class, we will always realize that they do not have the final claim to our allegiance; that above all lesser loyalties there remains one supreme loyalty, loyalty to that universal society of which Jesus the Christ is Lord.

And with an answer to our questions and an object for our devotion, faith in God gives us what we most need today: a comradeship which transcends all that is divisive in space and time and makes the man who enjoys it in a true sense a citizen of the world.

Thank God there are still living in the world people to whom faith in God means just this. You will find them in Germany among the members of the Confessional Synod. The Confessional Synod, you will remember, is that little group of courageous Protestant Christians who have refused to yield to Hitler's demand that the Church make the will of the state its supreme law. They are facing persecution of the most painful and trying character. They are denied freedom of speech and of communication. Their mail is censored, their telephone conversations overheard, and at any moment they may be taken from their homes and their parishes to the concentration camp. But they are sustained and kept steady by their faith in God as the ultimate reality with whom are the issues of life and in fellowship with whom is to be found the only enduring peace. This is typical of what is going on in many parts of the world today. There are people who, under conditions of persecution and strain sufficient to daunt the stoutest spirit, are sustained by their faith that God is real. You will find these people in Paris among the exiled Russians who, driven from the home of their birth, have found a new center of life in a foreign city, and in their little seminary in the Rue de Crimée are training the priests for what they confidently believe is to be the Church of the new Russia which is to be. You will find them in Manchukuo among those leaders of the Chinese church who overnight have been taken from their parishes and without trial confined in jail for the mere offense of being Christian. You will find them in Japan. Some of you have met recently one of them, that noble spirit, Kagawa, who, in an imperialistic age, has dared to stand, not only in word but in life, for the internationalism of the gospel.

Somehow it seems as if it took persecution to wake men to the sense of God. It was so in the early days of the Roman Empire when Christianity was a missionary religion and confession might mean martyrdom. It is still so in many parts of the world today.

4. WHY SOME PEOPLE FIND IT HARD TO REALIZE THE FACT OF GOD

What then are some of the reasons which make it hard for many of our contemporaries to realize God's presence?

One reason, a very obvious one, is that they are so busy that they have no time to think about him. Their day is so full of things to be done that there is no leisure left for quiet contemplation. Among the many distracting influences that compete today for their attention prayer is crowded out.

This is a real difficulty. But it is not insuperable. We can overcome it if we will, provided we take pains. However busy we are, we can always make room for the things that we regard as most important. But it takes resolution to do this, and, what is rarer still, ingenuity. We are the creatures of habit, and where our accepted calendar leaves no time for quiet we must form new habits to meet the new conditions.

A more basic reason why people do not find God when

they look for him is that they are looking for a kind of God who is not really there. They have formed a false picture of what God is like, and so they do not recognize him when they see him.

There are two reasons for this misconception. One is intellectual, and the other moral.

The intellectual reason for our failure to recognize God appears in the association of God's presence with something extraordinary, not to say magical, the kind of experience that underlay the belief in miracle in its older form. When we think of God primarily as the great wonder-worker, we shall not be apt to recognize his presence in the familiar world of law with which science is concerned. And yet this world too is God's world and he is speaking to us through it.

I do not mean of course that God is not present in the exceptional as well as in the familiar aspects of our world, or that wonder has no place in our approach to him. To do this would be to be false to the religious experience of those whose contact with God has been most frequent and most assured. But I do mean that the God whom religion reveals to us is the God of all life and that when we have found him at any one point the surest proof that we are right will be that now that we have found him we shall recognize his presence everywhere.

More serious is the moral reason for our failure to find God. This grows out of the assumption that God is a being who has his favorites and who rewards them with prosperity. It is the kind of misconception into which the Psalmist fell when he said: "I have been young, and now am old; yet have I not seen the righteous forsaken, nor his seed begging bread." [3]   God, to those who think of him in this way, is one who evidences his presence through the immediate deliverance of his worshiper from the evils which beset him in any one of the countless forms which they assume: sickness, suffering, disappointment, poverty, the loss of friends, the frustration of ambition.

Now here again I would not be misunderstood. The God whom Christians called "Father" does help his children in their needs. But that help must come in his way, not in ours. And often it comes to us in ways that we find it hard to recognize, and after long delay. In our world, hard as it may be to explain, evil is no monopoly of the wicked. The righteous too have their share of it. Indeed many of them will tell us that it has proved to them the most direct means of access to God. It is not when things go well that we are most conscious of God. Often it is just our sense of being forsaken that opens our eyes to the place where God is really at work. Evil is a two-edged sword. It may mean the death of hope. But it may also mean, thank God, the stimulus which reveals to us our own inadequacy and leads us to look beyond ourselves for help.

Both of these misconceptions have a common root— namely, a wrong idea of what God is and how he reveals himself. They may be valid against some ways of conceiving of God, but not against the real God with whom vital religion makes us acquainted.

[3] Psalm 37: 25.

But even when we have freed ourselves from these misconceptions and have learned from those who have found God before us what God is like, there remains a serious difficulty, the difficulty which is due to the fact that, unlike nature and man, God has no definite physical embodiment through which we can make him real to the senses.

To our materialistic age, accustomed to test reality by the mathematical standard of exact measurement, this often seems an insuperable difficulty. Yet when more carefully examined it will be found that it too rests upon a misconception—the misconception, namely, that we reach God only when we leave nature and man behind.

So long as nature was thought of as a little island surrounded by the shoreless ocean of the supernatural, it was natural to think of God in this way. But today our conception of nature has expanded in such immeasurable ways that if we are to put God out of nature we shall have to push him so far away that contact will be all but impossible. When we speak, and rightly, of the transcendence of God, we do not mean that God is absent from nature any more than we mean that the spirit of man is absent from his body. We mean that the God who is present in nature is different from nature. He is present in nature as the spirit of man is present in his body, as the directing and controlling principle without which all that the physical instrument does would be meaningless and ineffectual.

When we have once come to see this, our difficulty in finding God is seen to lie at the opposite pole. It is not that God has no physical embodiment, no language of sense, by which he can speak to us, but that he has so many. He is speaking to us every day, and we are touching him every day; but we do not recognize his voice because we are looking for him outside of nature and so we fail to see that nature is the instrument which he is using for his self-revelation.

5. WHERE GOD MAKES HIS PRESENCE EVIDENT TO-DAY

Where then are we to look for God today? I might say anywhere, and it would be true. For God, as we have seen, is everywhere. But this answer, though true, is not helpful. It is too general. We must have some more definite answer, something which enables us to choose between the enticing possibilities that are offered to us.

Such an answer is not hard to find. It has been suggested to us by our preliminary definition. We should look for God in whatever in nature or in human life gives the answer to our ultimate questions, sets the standard for our moral endeavor, or supplies the inner satisfaction which gives joy to life and inspiration to service; in a word, to whatever translates our life from a succession of blind and meaningless events into a meaningful and valuable whole. When we have found this we shall have found God.

When we enter upon our quest in this spirit we shall find that there are many things that are doing this for us and are doing it every day. In particular, God is to be found (1) in nature conceived as a system of things that conserves and promotes moral values; (2) in our own better self; (3) in the great traditions of our race; but supremely and above all for us Christians (4) in the person of Jesus Christ.

In the past it has been customary for theologians to begin with the first of these ways of approach and to make nature, in the comprehensive sense in which science studies it, our point of contact with God.

And there is much to be said for this way of procedure. It is true that God speaks to us through nature, and that through nature he is teaching us lessons that we need to learn. He is speaking to us through our consciousness of dependence, not simply in physical things, but in our moral life; through the discovery that no one of us is an isolated individual, but that we are all parts of a single system, so that when we violate a law, whether it be in the physical realm or in the moral, the consequence follows as inevitably as the rising and the setting of the sun. He is speaking to us through the uses that nature serves, the way in which all the parts of the complicated machine we call nature work together for ends that mind can set for itself and will can execute. Through nature God is teaching us lessons of order, of discipline, of the subordination of the part to the whole, and of the present to the future. Above all, God is speaking to us through the beauty of nature, the harmony of form and color that is at once the inspiration and the despair of the artist as he tries to reproduce in verse or in color the "light that never was on sea or land."

John Oxenham, in his little group of poems called "The Sacraments of Nature," [4] has put into words this unique

---

[4] By permission.

quality of nature by which, though itself speechless, it
lends itself to the uses of man:

"Kneel always when you light a fire!
Kneel reverently, and thankful be
For God's unfailing charity,
And on the ascending flame inspire
A little prayer, that shall upbear
The incense of your thankfulness
For this sweet grace
    Of warmth and light!
For here again is sacrifice
    For your delight.

Within the wood,
    That lived a joyous life
Through sunny days and rainy days
    And winter storms and strife;
.   .   .   .
Within the coal,
    Where forests lie entombed,
Oak, elm, and chestnut, beech and red pine bole—
    God shrined his sunshine, and enwombed
For you these stores of light and heat,
Your life-joys to complete.
These all have died that you might live;
Yours now the high prerogative,
    To loose their long captivities—
To give them new sweet span of life
    And fresh activities.

Kneel always when you light a fire!
Kneel reverently,
And grateful be
To God for his unfailing charity!"

But while nature speaks to us in all these ways, it is never clearly. What she gives us is intimations, suggestions, prophecies. To meet God convincingly we must turn to the second of the ways in which he is speaking to us—namely, the better self in each one of us.

God is speaking to us in that restless monitor that we call the voice of conscience, or, if that be too old-fashioned a word, the sense of value—all that we sum up in the words "duty" or "honor" or "self-respect," the thing in us that will not let us permanently be satisfied with second best, but holds before us always as an end, even if an end forever unattainable, the ideal of perfection.

And even when he is not felt as speaking directly—and there are many in our day who do not feel this sense of a direct presence, and some of them among the most sensitive in their appreciation of the good—God is yet speaking indirectly in the sense of loneliness and dissatisfaction which is the natural result of his absence. How will you account for the great increase of suicide in our time if it be not due to the loneliness of a generation which, having lost God out of its consciousness, finds no strength adequate to support the strain of modern life, with its insecurity and disillusionment?

Above all, God is speaking to us in the appeal of human love, which is the central and recurrent message of conscience through the centuries: the discovery that there are others who have a right to our regard as well as we, human personalities with hopes and aspirations and capacities, whose lives are thwarted because they lack the opportunity of self-expression which has been granted to us. He is speaking to us in that spirit of hope which refuses to make the past the measure of the future, which finds no failure insuperable and no obstacle unsurmountable, but is willing to meet even those who persecute and revile us with the love that can forgive not once, but unto seventy times seven.

But this inner voice, essential and commanding as it may be, has its limitations. It does not always speak with equal clarity, and even when it has spoken to us we find that to others it seems to bring a different message. We face a world in which those who are sincere Christians often honestly disagree. What should we do in a situation like this?

Here help comes to us from the third of the three ways in which God is making his presence known to us today, through the institutions and literature that gather up for us that which is best in the experience of the past and the personalities that inspire and direct them.

That means for us Christians that he speaks to us through the Bible, through the Church, and most clearly of all through the great personality to whom Bible and Church alike point, Jesus Christ, in whom his disciples in every age have seen God's clearest word to man.

First of all through the Bible. I suppose that that is the way in which we first thought of God as speaking to us at all. The Bible, we were taught as children, was the Word of God, his direct message to our race about his nature and will. And at first we took that message very literally, like a constitution which might be put forth by a government or a letter which a father might write to his child.

But as we grew older and came to know the Bible better we came to see that God's way of speaking to us through the Bible was not so simple. It was his message, to be sure, but it came to us through the lips of men to whom he had already spoken, and their assurance that it was God with whom they had to do gave added force to the message. It was not a bolt out of the blue. It was the witness of men who had experienced God's presence and passed on to us the discovery of what that presence had meant to them. "O taste and see that the Lord is good." [5] "No good thing will be he withhold from them that walk uprightly." [6] "I can do all things through Christ which strengtheneth me." [7] Here is a note that we find recurrent in the Bible and which gives it its human as well as its divine quality.

So we are led naturally from the Bible to the Church as another of the ways in which God is speaking to us today. For the Church is simply our name for the company of people who have heard God speak and who are trying to live by what they hear. No doubt there are many who have not heard clearly, and others who have forgotten what once they heard. The Church, as a great Christian once said, is a *corpus permixtum,* a composite body in which we find inextricably intermingled the evil and the good. The fact remains that with all its faults the Church preserves the great tradition of the race and is today a ceaseless reminder not only of what God has said in the past but what he is saying today.

[5] Psalm 34: 8.   [6] Psalm 84: 11.   [7] Philippians 4: 13.

And this is true of the Church in both of the aspects in which we have been considering it; as a company of people witnessing to us of the new life which has come to them through Christ and as an institution mediating by the objective forms of liturgy and sacrament the content of the historic gospel. It is through the lives of the great Christians who most completely incarnate the spirit of the divine love that we gain our clearest intimation of what God is like. It is through the historic practices that gather up in symbolic acts the meaning of these many individual experiences—above all, through the most intimate and personal of the Christian sacraments, the Eucharist or Lord's Supper—that we become vividly conscious of an unseen presence lending joy and meaning to life.

Bible and Church alike point us to Jesus as the one who sums up in most definite and concise form the meaning of what God has been saying to his people through the centuries. Jesus, to our Christian faith, is God's supreme self-revelation, his living and life-giving Word. In Jesus we find not only the comrade and teacher and master and friend we need, we find something that we need even more than these. We find a symbol which from generation to generation interprets to us that which is deepest in the heart and mind of God.

And by a symbol I mean something which gives definite and driving force to that which apart from it we might dimly suspect but could not clearly visualize.

When I contrast Jesus with nature and with conscience I do not mean that he is to be added to these as something independent and separate. I mean that Jesus is the one without whom they could not do for us all, or the best, that they were meant to do. If we ask how we come to know that there was such a being as Jesus at all, the answer is, through the contacts of sense that nature makes possible—what we have heard of him with our ears, what we have read of him with our eyes, what has been visualized for us in the elaborate symbols of ritual and sacrament by which the Church has tried to make his personality real.

But all that sense does for us in this way would be of no avail if there were not something in us to which the message answers, that inner voice of conscience which is the most intimate and personal of all the ways of making God real. It is because, when we meet Jesus, he seems no longer a stranger, but the one for whom we have been unconsciously waiting, the one who reveals to us, as we could not otherwise have discovered it, what in our heart of hearts we know we ought to be. It is, in a word, because when we meet Jesus we discover for the first time that which answers to what is deepest in ourselves, that he becomes to us in the truest sense God's Word to us; no longer simply a man among men, but God manifest in the flesh for our salvation.

One lesson in particular Jesus teaches us which without the help of his example it would be hard for us to learn—namely, that of the presence of God in suffering. It is not when the sky is brightest that we see God most clearly, but when the shadows lengthen and the night falls, the night of man's ultimate mystery, the mystery of pain.

Among the letters of Baron von Hügel, that saintly Roman Catholic writer and thinker, there is one written to Mr. Gladstone's daughter on the death of her father after an illness which had brought him much suffering. Having paid a tribute to all that the great English statesman had done throughout his life of unusual activity, Baron von Hügel concludes with these remarkable words: "I have always loved to think of devoted suffering as the highest, purest, perhaps the only quite pure form of action: and so it was a special grace that one as devoted and as active as your father, should have been allowed and strengthened to practise the most devoted action possible for a sentient and rational creature of God." [8]

No one but a Christian could have written that letter. No one who had not passed with Jesus through the dark valley, and come out into the sunshine, would have dared to speak of great suffering as a gracious gift of God.

Yet this is a lesson that the greatest Christians have learned from Jesus—Jesus who through the bitter experiences of the Garden and the Cross drank the cup of suffering to the dregs, of whom we read that "for the joy that was set before him" he "endured the cross, despising the shame, and is set down at the right hand of the throne of God." [9]

5. WHAT TO DO WITH WHAT WE FIND

There is then no lack of ways in which God is speaking to us today, no lack of places where to the eye of faith his presence is manifest. All that is needed is an attentive mind, a heart at leisure from itself. Prayer is the

[8] von Hügel, F., *Selected Letters* (1896-1924), ed. by B. Holland (London, 1927), p. 70.
[9] Hebrews 12: 2.

[131]

way in which this contact is made, and mind and heart become responsive to the fact of God.

But here we meet the fact that for many Christians of our time the practice of prayer has largely fallen into disuse. I do not know how it is in the South, but for us in the North there are many homes where family prayer is no longer practiced, and even the habit of daily personal prayer is sadly in abeyance. There are many reasons for this with which I have tried to deal in a book which may have fallen into the hands of some of you.[10] The fact remains that the sense of God is not real today for many of our fellow Christians, and with the loss of the sense of God the sense of the importance and of the practicability of prayer is apt to go.

Our first responsibility, then, as ministers is to win men to a new sense of the importance of prayer, and for this there is no better way than to confront them with tasks too great for man's unaided strength.

Here the difficulties of our time may prove our best helper, for they force upon us the contrast between the divine ideal and our human capacity. Unless there are reserves on which we can draw, our hope of realizing the ideals to which the gospel commits us seems vain. So, I repeat, I know no better place for the minister to begin in his effort to help his parishioners to recover the lost habit of prayer than with the difficulties and dangers of the time in which we live. One may dispense with prayer for one's self, but when one attempts seriously to take up the bur-

[10] Brown, W. Adams, *The Life of Prayer in a World of Science* (New York, 1931).

dens of others' lives, one feels the need of larger resources than one's own unaided strength can provide.

Will you pardon a word of personal testimony? As I try to recollect the times when my own devotional life has been most keen and vivid, I find that it has been in the hours when I have been preparing to conduct morning worship in the Seminary chapel. As I have tried to make real to myself the lives of the young men whom I was trying to help, their difficulties, their problems, their temptations, their glorious possibilities, I have found familiar words of scripture glow with a new meaning and come to realize afresh that the Bible is in truth what I had often told my students in words that it was—the most modern of all books.

So I have no doubt you have found it in your own experience. As you have looked forward to the morning service and thought of the lives entrusted by God to your pastoral care, you have felt your own sense of his presence quickened, and out of your very helplessness and limitation have won a new conviction of the infinite resources in God waiting to be drawn upon by your faith.

In much the same way it seems to me we must try to make prayer real to our people. Prayer is not given to us selfishly for our comfort. It is the means through which we are made strong and wise for service. It was this even to our Lord himself. You remember his words in the high-priestly prayer: "For their sakes I sanctify myself." [11] To help others I set myself apart. If for him, how much more for us must ethics and religion go together?

[11] John 17: 19.

On the technique of prayer I cannot take time to speak here further than to say that there is a technique and that it must be mastered. There is much here to be learned from Catholic books of devotion, much, too, from the recent Protestant literature on the subject. It is surprising how many principles of modern psychology have been anticipated by the old saints. Almost all that is true in this psychology, I have often told my students, is to be found in the spiritual exercises of Saint Ignatius Loyola: the principle of relaxation, for example, and the principle of recollection, the principle of repetition and the principle of variation, the place of interest, and the help furnished by posture—all these are matters where helpful counsel can be given by one who has made himself familiar with the best literature of the subject. Professor Hocking, for example, in his great book, *The Meaning of God in Human Experience*,[12] has much to say of the principle of rhythm in the religious life, the help that comes to us by alternating periods of quiet with periods of activity.

But the one thing that matters is that we should remember that there are three concerned in any Christian prayer: God, the self, and the fellow. We go into our closet and shut the door, not that we may enjoy a fellowship denied to others, but that through renewed contact with the God who is himself love, we may be purified and disciplined to do our part effectively in the life of the brotherhood.

You will understand now what I meant when I spoke of the minister's responsibility for the conduct of public worship as at once the most distinctive and the most re-

[12] Hocking, W. E., New Haven, 1912, pp. 405 seq.

sponsible of all his functions. May I add also, the one that confers the rarest privilege. For what comes to other Christians only incidentally and at odd moments—the privilege of mediating between God and man—is made possible for the minister with every passing week. With what eager anticipation, then, as the hour of service approaches, must he look forward to the moment when it shall be his privilege to lift the hearts of his people in united prayer to God and invite them to the act of consecration in which all great prayer culminates.

For on this all those who have been masters of the art of prayer are agreed, that the one sure test of genuine prayer is the act of consecration in which it issues. God makes his presence known with irresistible conviction in the act of the will by which man surrenders without reserve to the highest he knows.

I do not know how that summons will come to you. It may be in some sudden flash of insight coming to you out of the clear. It may be through some slow ripening of judgment, as you meet each day's duty as it comes. But this I know, that if you meet that summons with unreserved surrender there may be given to you that greatest of life's gifts, a God who can do for you more than you ask or even think, a God in whom you may find the answer to your ultimate questions, the object of your supreme devotion, and a companion in fellowship with whom you may find unfailing inspiration and enduring joy.

CHAPTER VI

THE MINISTER AS EVANGELIST: THE GOOD NEWS OF GOD'S PRESENCE IN HISTORY

1. THE MINISTER AS PREACHER OF A HISTORIC GOSPEL

2. DIFFERENT WAYS OF CONCEIVING GOD'S PRESENCE IN HISTORY

3. CONSEQUENCES FOR THE MINISTER'S WORK AS EVANGELIST. THE PROPHETIC NOTE IN THE MINISTER'S TEACHING

4. SOME PERMANENT CHRISTIAN CONVICTIONS CONCERNING GOD'S PRESENCE IN HISTORY

1. THE MINISTER AS PREACHER OF A HISTORIC GOSPEL

IN the discharge of his God-given task as witness for God the minister fulfills many functions. He is preacher, teacher, leader in worship, pastor, administrator, citizen. In all of these he must have but one aim—namely, to be true to his calling as a minister of the gospel and an interpreter of its message to men.

Paul summed up this message long ago in the words that God was in Christ reconciling the world unto himself and that he has committed unto us the word of reconciliation. But since there are many in our day to whom the Bible language is no longer familiar, we may translate Paul's language into more modern speech and say that the good news that we are charged to preach is the fact that God is in history and is therefore accessible; that he has shown us what he is like and is therefore recognizable; and that he invites us to share his purpose and is therefore imitable.

God is in history, and is therefore accessible. That is the beginning and end of our gospel. We are reminded of this by the name by which our religion is known, the name "Christian." This points us to a definite historic figure who is the object of our devotion and who invites us to test all rival gospels which claim men's allegiance by their relation to the revelation which he himself has brought.

This intimate connection with history is for Christians both an asset and a liability. It is an asset in that it furnishes the minister with a definite standard to which he can refer. It is a liability in that like all that is historical it requires trained intelligence to distinguish fact from fiction and to lay a firm basis for faith in assured and dependable data. The minister who is to do justice to the Christian gospel must be in the best sense of that word an educated man. He is to be an interpreter, and that means that he must be a student. And study is hard work and requires discipline not only of mind but of the sympathies and of the will.

This assured basis in history, I repeat, is an asset. What gives these rival gospels their appeal is the fact that they confront men with what is going on in the world today. They offer them a cause that is definite and accessible. They invite them to a comradeship in which they are asked to share responsibility. Well, our gospel can do the same. We, too, can point men to what is going on in the world today—a historic process which began long ago, to be sure, but which is still going on. We, too, can invite them to a comradeship in which they are asked to share responsibility. They are to be helpers of God in his great task of making—let me say rather, of remaking—men.

But the fact that our gospel is a historic gospel may be a liability as well as an asset. For we are not at the end, but at the beginning of our responsibility when we have affirmed God's presence in history. There is more than one way of conceiving of that presence, and there is no point on which the difference between Christians has been more pronounced or has had more far-reaching consequences.

2. DIFFERENT WAYS OF CONCEIVING GOD'S PRESENCE IN HISTORY

There is, for example, the familiar difference between the Catholic and the Protestant interpretation of history. The Catholic finds God present in a continuous stream of tradition of which the pope is spokesman and interpreter; the Protestant concentrates attention on the Bible as the book in which God has brought together, once for all, all that is necessary for man's salvation, faith, and life.

It is true that when we examine this contrast more carefully it proves to be less extreme than is often supposed. All Catholics agree that, while tradition must be added to the Bible, the Bible remains in the highest sense normative and nothing can be Christian which contradicts its teaching. Protestants on their part agree that God's presence in history did not stop with the Bible, but that he is still at work in his world through his Holy Spirit; and they have recorded their understanding of that work in creeds which have become in fact, if not in theory, a tradition with normative authority.

There is, however, another contrast which cuts even

deeper. It is that which grows out of differing views of the way in which God makes his presence known. One view makes the sharpest possible contrast between God's supernatural activities in revelation and redemption and the ordinary processes of his providence which the Calvinists are accustomed to describe as common grace. According to this view God is pictured as outside his world, intervening from time to time by miracle or special grace, but for the most part leaving things to take their course as they are acted upon by the second causes with which God endowed nature at its creation or the free will which is the distinctive (yet, alas, often the fatal) prerogative of man.

Within this general framework there is room for wide differences of understanding. Interpretations vary all the way from the Catholic view, which sees in the organized church, and specifically in the priesthood and sacraments, the convincing proof of God's presence in history, to the view of evangelical Protestantism, which finds in dramatic conversions of the Jerry McAuley type the clearest evidence that God is at work in the world. The most striking example of what we may call the catastrophic conception of God's presence in history is the premillennial view that would have us concentrate all of our attention upon the imminent physical coming of Christ to establish his Kingdom on earth in a restored Jerusalem. Unfortunately, those who commend to us this view are themselves divided in their interpretation of the Biblical prophecies and of the differing chronological schemes to which these differing interpretations have given rise.

In contrast to views of this kind which make much of crisis is the view which identifies the presence of God in history with those long-time processes through which in the course of the centuries his purpose is being progressively made clear. This evolutionary view of God's presence, optimistic in its general outlook, was much in evidence in theological circles a generation ago. In contrast to exaggerated doctrines of total depravity liberal theologians revived the ancient saying of Tertullian about the soul that is by nature Christian and eagerly welcomed the evolutionary doctrines of men like Spencer and Fiske as giving us our most authentic account of the way God was making his presence evident in history.

The years that have passed have brought their disillusioning experiences. With the War and its aftermath in the present armed peace, our dream of an early coming of the Kingdom of God by the simple process of growth has been rudely shattered. Our mood today is like that of those disciples on the Emmaus Road who, when the Master questioned them as to what had been happening in Jerusalem, added to their sad story of the crucifixion the revealing words: "But we trusted that it had been he who should have redeemed Israel." We trusted, but it seems we were mistaken.

The words might almost be taken as a paraphrase of Reinhold Niebuhr's widely read book, *Moral Man and Immoral Society*. We liberals, he tells us in this book, have trusted in the power of reason and of love to bring in the Kingdom. We trusted, but it seems we were mistaken.

To many who are in this mood today a rereading of the Bible should bring encouragement rather than despair. What has come upon us is no strange or unexpected thing. It is only what our Master warned us would happen if we forsook the way to which he pointed and followed our own devices in selfishness and pride.

Many years ago in China I met an old boatman who had been converted to Christianity in middle life. I was interested to learn what it was which led to his conversion. He told me that the first thing that excited his curiosity was the work of the Christian doctors who went about healing the sick without hope of reward. He could not understand why they did it, so he went to church to learn the Christian doctrine. And the first sermon he heard was about the Flood. This, he told me, made a very favorable impression upon him, for, he said, "I had myself experienced the flood, and so I knew that the doctrine was true."

I have often thought since that the words of that old boatman give us a very sound doctrine of Biblical inspiration. The Bible is God's book to us, not because it tells us what happened in the world long ago, but because it tells us what is happening in the world today and what may happen to us. Well, we too have experienced the deluge and when we open our Bibles we find that it is the same kind of catastrophe which came upon Israel in the days of the prophets and that the causes which have brought it upon us are the same causes which brought it upon them.

I remember vividly a conversation with a distinguished Swiss professor just after the conclusion of the World War

He was telling me how, as he sat in his study at Zürich and heard the sounds of the shells breaking just across the border and realized what they must mean to the young men in the trenches, it seemed to him that he could no longer believe in God. And then, he said, I opened my Bible and in the pages of Israel's prophets I learned that they too had been through just such experiences as I was going through and that in and through the very desolation of their time they had discovered God at work in his righteousness and in his love.

It is an experience which is happening to many in our time. But there are many to whom it has not yet happened, many who need the inspiration and enlightenment that can only come to them from you.

3. CONSEQUENCES FOR THE MINISTER'S WORK AS EVANGELIST. THE PROPHETIC NOTE IN THE MINISTER'S TEACHING

It is no light and easy task then to which I invite you when I summon you to take seriously your responsibility as evangelists. It is a task which will make demand upon every power you possess, not simply for the impartial recognition of fact, which is the mark of the scientist, but for that deeper insight into the meaning of fact which is the contribution of the theologian.

We hear much in these days about the prophetic function of the minister, but prophecy in the sense in which the word is used in the Bible is not concerned primarily with the future, but with the present. It is the discovery in the midst of the confused and baffling conditions of the time of the Living God at work in his world. That is what gave significance to the teaching of Israel's prophets, and makes their message as applicable to our own day as it was to theirs. They were interpreters, to those who were content to live upon the surface of things, of those eternal principles of justice and mercy that are true in every age. That is why their teachings can never be outgrown.

To appreciate the full significance of the prophetic teaching we must put it in its setting: not merely its immediate historical setting in the story of Israel's religion, but the larger history of which that story is a part. In contrast to the Eastern religions which preceded Christianity, Hinduism and Buddhism, where the ideal was flight from the world through the suppression of individuality, whether that suppression was conceived, as in Brahmanism, as union with the Absolute through inward contemplation, or, as in Buddhism, as the attainment of Nirvana through the death of desire, the religion of Israel was ethical monotheism. The ideal which it held up before its followers was not the suppression of desire, but the discipline of the will to a higher obedience.

At first this teaching took the form of a doctrine of election. God, who had made man for himself, had chosen a people to be the object of his special care and the channel through which his revelation was to be mediated to other nations. But there was a condition which must be fulfilled. If Israel was to receive the blessings God had in store for it, it must be true to the standard he required. Its people must be righteous, as God was righteous, and when in willfulness or pride they forgot the divine requirement and became oppressors of the poor he visited their sin with its appropriate punishment.[1]

This conception of a moral purpose of God in history is the presupposition of the prophetic teaching. From the first the religion of Israel had been a social religion in the sense that the unit with which it dealt was the nation, rather than the individuals who composed it; but it had been a local religion. Its vision was bounded by Canaan, and the great world that lay beyond was all but unknown. The prophets commanded a broader horizon. They first measured the extent and the completeness of Jehovah's control. Not Israel only was subject to his will, but the great world powers—Egypt, Assyria, Persia, with whose fortune that of Israel was inextricably involved. All the movements of contemporary history—the march of contending armies, the rise of dynasties, and the fall of cities—took place by his decree and for the execution of his purpose. The Assyrian was the rod of his anger,[2] the razor with which he was to shave the head and beard.[3] Egypt was his servant.[4] Philistia and Syria were executors of his will.[5] Far from the misfortunes of Israel proving that God had abandoned them, they were rather warnings which he had sent them for their good, stages which they must pass on their journey to salvation. The great thing was to understand their meaning, and to learn the lessons which they were designed to teach.

[1] In this and the following pages I have used some paragraphs from my book, *Is Christianity Practicable?* (New York, 1916). Cf. especially pp. 55-58, 60, 64-66, 68, 70-78.
[2] Isaiah 10: 5.
[3] Isaiah 7: 20.
[4] Isaiah 19: 19-25.
[5] Isaiah 9: 11, 12.

Christianity inherited Israel's faith in an all-encompassing Providence. It gave this faith new significance through its new revelation of God's character and of his redemptive purpose made known through Jesus Christ. It shifted the emphasis from the outward drama of the army and the camp to the inward struggle of the soul. It spiritualized and universalized the social ideal; and through the resurrection faith opened vistas of comfort and hope beyond the grave, which were not available in the earlier stages of Israel's history. But it never wavered in its faith in God as Lord of all; of this life as well as of the life to come; of evil as well as of good; of nations as well as of the individuals who compose them.

This confidence was the result of no shallow optimism. When all goes smoothly it is easy to speak and to think comfortably. Some of us have learned this to our cost. We had underestimated the forces which resist progress. We had supposed that the great prize for which we had been contending was to be quickly won; that war on a great scale belonged to the past, and that our more enlightened age, in spite of its underlying selfishness and cruelty, could somehow slip easily into the Kingdom of God. We have had a rude awakening, and we are tempted to go to the opposite extreme and to wonder whether, after all, our contemporary pessimists are not right, and our ideal of a social order at once just and free is not an idle dream.

Our predecessors in the faith were under no such illusion. If they believed in peace, it was not because they were unacquainted with war. There is no fact which confronts us today, however appalling and terrible, which they had not looked in the face. If they believed in God's control of history, it was not because they underestimated the forces of evil, but because they had confidence that God was able to overrule evil for good.

It is worth while to recall these familiar facts, because they will help us to keep our sense of balance and proportion. We speak of our experience as unparalleled in human history, and there is a sense in which this is true. But the statement needs qualification. The present crisis is unparalleled in magnitude, but not in quality. Hunger is hunger, and pain pain, and death death the world over; in Palestine as in Spain, in Rome as in Austria and France. And the anguish of hope deferred, the shattering of ideals, the bitterness of the "I would, but ye would not," were as poignant to the martyrs and saints of the first Christian century as they can be to us today. There is nothing, I repeat, that any man or woman or child is experiencing today which has not been experienced by others over and over again. There is no challenge to faith in what we see which has not been met by faith in the past and vanquished.

What Amos and Isaiah and Jeremiah were to the men of their own generation, that we modern preachers are called to be to the men of our own. We are to be interpreters of the meaning of what is happening to our world by the clue which is given to us by the revelation God has made of himself in Jesus Christ.

4. SOME PERMANENT CHRISTIAN CONVICTIONS CONCERING GOD'S PRESENCE IN HISTORY

What then do we see as Christians when we survey the story of the centuries that have preceded us? What do we foresee as we look forward to the untraveled road that lies ahead?

This first: We see God as the unseen actor in all that happens, guiding his world to the consummation which in his wisdom he has foreseen. We see him at work not as bare power, imposing his will by arbitrary decree, but as ethical personality having respect for human freedom, and relying for the ultimate triumph of his cause upon its appeal to that which is best in man.

We see God present in history as judge, bringing all that is done, whether in individual lives or in the life of nations, to the inexorable test of his law of love; and where that law is violated, from whatever cause, we see the violation visited with its unescapable consequences.

When we realize this we shall not be surprised at what is happening in our world today, nor shall we be dismayed. It is what we must expect if God be really the kind of God in whom Jesus Christ has taught us to believe.

The first lesson, then, that comes to us as Christians when we contemplate the sufferings of the present is that of the need of self-examination and penitence. These great evils have not come upon mankind without a cause, and it is our duty, so far as we can, to understand this cause, that we may do our part to remove it.

One of the encouraging features of the present situation is that it has put the moral issue again in the center of attention. We had been told that mankind had outgrown the sense of sin, but today we see it revived in the most unexpected quarters. It gives its tragic interest to the discussion of war guilt, so dramatically revived by Germany's denunciation of the Treaty of Versailles. It is implicit in the debate between communist and capitalist as to who is responsible for the evils from which the present world is suffering. Radically as the disputants may differ in the remedy which they propose for our present disaster, there is one thing in which they are agreed. And that is that they are fighting to uphold the elemental principles of justice and morality against men who have banded themselves together for purposes of selfishness and greed. It is not we who are responsible, so all alike assert. But that there has been guilt on a colossal scale, all are greed. What is this but a confession that the sense of sin is still alive in men and the old questions of guilt and punishment are living questions?

But the Bible not only points out to us the inevitable connection between sin and suffering. It shows us also what is the root of all our misery. This sin is unbrotherliness. It is the self-centered life, regarding only its own interests and indifferent to the needs and sufferings of others, which in every age has been the spring of social jealousy and social unrest. What the Assyrians planned to do to Israel as a whole, individual Israelites, relying on their superior advantages of birth, or place, or wealth, had done in effect to their less fortunate fellow countrymen. They had treated them as the raw material of their own pleasure and gain. They had ignored their rights as human beings—common children of a common father—to a life that was full and free. The national misery which involved their own fortunes with those whom they had despised and oppressed was the natural and inevitable consequence of the national sin.

What was true then is true now. Trace any one of the major evils of our time to its cause, and you will come at last to some form of selfishness, individual or national. Whatever during all the years that have gone has sown envy and distrust between individuals and nations; wherever the weak have been oppressed and the longing for freedom has been stifled; wherever men have thought basely of their fellows, attributing to them conduct and desires which they would despise in themselves; wherever brute force has been magnified as the supreme reality, and the power of love has been belittled or denied; wherever, in short, individuals and nations calling themselves Christian have denied by their conduct the religion they profess, there they have been laying the train which was some day destined to explode in bitterness and hate. As certainly as day follows night, so certainly disaster follows sin. It is futile to cry, Peace, Peace, when there is no peace. It is idle to expect peace where the causes which produce war remain unremoved.

It is not theologians and preachers only who have been saying this. It is being said even more forcibly by economists and statesmen. There is a long line of witnesses whom I might summon to testify if there were time—men like Sir Arthur Salter, Financial Adviser to the League of Nations, or Owen Young, the author of "The Young

Plan." These men have been telling us for years that unless we changed our habits and began to take seriously the crucial fact that we are in the most literal sense of the term members of one another our civilization is doomed. On a recent visit to this country Sir George Paish, the English economist, declared to an audience of society women in New York that unless we begin to apply the principles of the Christian religion to the solution of our financial and economic problems he saw no hope for the world.

"I am no Christian," George Bernard Shaw is reported to have said, "any more than Pilate was. But after sixty years of study of human affairs, I see no way out of our present troubles but the way Jesus Christ would have taken if he had undertaken the work of a practical statesman."

Yes, God is present in our world as judge. That is the first thing we must say to our contemporaries. But that is only one-half of our message. There is another, even more important. God is present in our world as Redeemer, using the very pathos and tribulation of our time to win men to himself and to rekindle in their hearts the fire of an unconquerable love.

Man's extremity is God's opportunity. It was so in the darkest days of Israel's history. Always there was the remnant to which the future belonged. It was so in the black hours that followed the Crucifixion. Easter came with its message of the living Christ. It was so in the days of Roman persecution. The seed of the martyrs has been the seed of the Church. It has been so through all the centuries. And it is still so today.

This explains the strange phenomenon, so baffling to faith, of the suffering of the innocent with the guilty. Always this has been the crux of the problem of suffering. It is not hard to understand suffering when there is sin. The mystery is rather on the other side, that so often the wicked seem to escape their just punishment. But that the righteous should suffer while the wicked go scot-free, this seems a challenge of God's moral government so staggering that for long, even in the face of the most convincing evidence, men refused to believe in the fact.

And yet it remains true that the innocent do suffer with and for the guilty and that the iniquities of the fathers are visited upon the children unto the third and fourth generation? What does it mean?

There are two things which it might mean. One is that the ultimate reality is force, and that the Christian faith in the loving Father, who cares for each one of his human children, is without foundation in fact. The other is that the individual is not the final unit; that because God's plan is social, a family, and not simply a collection of unrelated sons and daughters, his method of training must be more complex than would be the case if he were dealing with isolated individuals. It is the latter which is the Christian view. God's method is a method of redemptive love, and redemptive love can save only at the cost of vicarious suffering.

This is the Christian solution of the problem of problems, the suffering of the innocent with, and for, the guilty. It is the solution which finds its supreme example and seal in the Cross that was set up on Calvary.

But the cross has another and an even deeper meaning. It is the supreme revelation of a law that is valid everywhere and always, the law of the solidarity of all mankind in the moral life. It is not simply that Christ was *willing* to suffer for my sin. It is that, being what he was, he *could not but* suffer for it. When he became man it was not merely as an isolated individual, but as a member of the human family. He became involved in all the fortunes of the race, subject to that mysterious law of which we have spoken, that binds us all up together in one common bundle of life, so that not one of us can live for himself alone, but each is involved, for good or for evil, in the fortunes of all the rest.

How much this consciousness of human solidarity has been reinforced by the experiences through which the present generation has been passing! We have been learning in a terrible textbook the truth of the old words that God has "made of one every nation of men." We have seen war reaching beyond the nations immediately engaged, and laying its ruthless and destroying hands upon peace-loving and inoffensive people. There is not an island so remote but has felt the electric shock. There is not an individual so inconspicuous but on his shoulder some new burden has been laid as a direct result of the World War. The time has gone by when any nation can say to other nations: "It is no concern of yours what I do to my neighbor." For good or for evil (for evil certainly if not for good) we are members one of another. We have been told it before. We know it now.

But there is another side to this matter of human solidarity which it is just as important for us to understand, and that is its function as an agent of salvation. We have learned that there is a divine law which involves us all alike in the consequences of past sin. We have yet to learn that the same law may be made equally effective in the transmission of good.

And yet this, too, is the lesson of the cross. There is a contagion of good as well as of evil. As the sin of mankind brought suffering to the innocent Christ, necessarily, and as part of God's law, so the courageous acceptance of that suffering by Christ brought salvation to sinful mankind, with an equal necessity, and as part of a law equally divine. In redemption, as in suffering, Christ is the type of humanity at its best. What was true of him on the supreme scale, and in exceptional degree, may be true on a lesser scale, but no less truly in the case of every man or woman who follows him in his path of loving sacrifice and has learned from the heart to pray his prayer after him, "Father, forgive them; for they know not what they do." [6] Paul filling up on his part "that which is behind of the afflictions of Christ . . . for his body's sake, which is the Church," [7] Latimer bidding the faltering Ridley "Be of good comfort and play the man," since "we shall light such a candle by God's grace in England as, I trust, shall never be put out," are but the most conspicuous examples of the great company of every name and age who, having followed Christ in his sufferings, have shared with him also the triumph of sacrificial love.

[6] Luke 23: 34.
[7] Colossians 1: 24.

Here, too, we find the teaching of the Bible corroborated by what is happening before our own eyes. We find its confirmation in Russia, where the fiery trial which has befallen the Church has raised up a new generation of priests who in their modest seminary in the Rue de Crimée in Paris are fitting themselves to play their part in the new and better Russian church in whose coming they confidently believe. We find it in Germany, where no threat of prison or concentration camp has been able to daunt the valiant band who are holding aloft the banner of Christ's gospel of universal love. We find it in Japan, where Kagawa, undaunted by the rising tide of militarism by which he is surrounded, preaches the gospel of the cooperative commonwealth. We find it in India, where, after all these centuries, the iron wall of caste is at last beginning to give way and the Untouchables to claim their rights as men. We see it in our own country where through all our blundering and ineffectiveness we see the nation as a whole facing our unchristian social order and feeling its way after a worthier and more Christian solution.

Yes, God is present in his world as Redeemer. That is what we see as we look with Christ's eyes upon the world. That is the good news which it is our privilege to preach to all those who are fearful because of the things they see coming upon the world.

CHAPTER VII

THE MINISTER AS TEACHER. WHAT TO TEACH AND HOW

1. THE DECLINE OF THE TEACHING OFFICE IN PROTESTANTISM

2. THE CHRISTIAN FACTS AS SUBJECT OF TEACHING

3. THE CHRISTIAN GOSPEL AS SUBJECT OF TEACHING

4. THE CHRISTIAN CHURCH AS SUBJECT OF TEACHING

5. SOME PRACTICAL DIFFICULTIES AND HOW TO MEET THEM

6. HOW THE NEEDS OF THE PUPILS DETERMINE THE METHOD OF THE TEACHER

Chapter VII

1. THE DECLINE OF THE TEACHING OFFICE IN PROT-
ESTANTISM

THE insight that God has been from the first and is even now active in history gives dignity to an aspect of the minister's work which has always received prominence in Protestantism, his work as a teacher. Teaching, to be sure, is not the only phase of the minister's work as an evangelist; but as Protestantism conceives it, it is, save one, the most important. The priestly relation alone (and I use the word in the good Protestant sense, to denote the work of the minister in helping his brother men to realize their spiritual relationship to their common Father)—the priestly relation alone is more important, and this depends for its full success upon the other. For Protestantism claims for every individual the right and the duty of direct access to God. The most that his fellow man can do (whether he be minister or layman) is to point the way, and for this he must know where God is to be found and what he is like when one has found him. Hence Protestantism, just because it has so high an estimate of the value and responsibility of the human soul, magnifies the teaching office of the minister, or, for that matter, of every Christian.

It is difficult, then, to exaggerate the importance of the minister's function as a teacher. Yet am I wrong in saying that of all the various aspects of the minister's work, this, in our modern Protestantism, has been the most neglected? The minister is many things in the modern world, and he is becoming new things every day. He is not only pastor, preacher, leader of worship, but executive, financier, promoter, organizer, club leader, social reformer, and I know not what all beside. But how many ministers can you name who, in the full meaning of that word, deserve to be called by the name that was most commonly addressed to Jesus—*teacher?*

It was not so in the older Protestantism. No part of the minister's work was deemed more important than the systematic instruction of his people. A minister's preaching in the course of the year covered all the great themes of the Christian gospel and all the major aspects of the Christian experience. Indeed, many of the best-known doctrinal treatises of the older Protestantism were given to the congregation in the form of sermons. I have in my library a majestic quarto of some seven hundred pages by a London minister named Thomas Watson. It is called A BODY OF PRACTICAL DIVINITY and consists, as the title quaintly puts it, of "176 SERMONS ON THE SHORTER CATECHISM COMPOSED BY THE REVEREND ASSEMBLY OF DIVINES AT WESTMINSTER." The date of the series is 1797. They believed in giving good measure in those days.

Times have changed since then. The catechism has long ago dropped out of fashion, and nothing equally effective has been devised to take its place. The Sunday school holds the children for one short hour a week and depends for the most part upon the services of voluntary and ill-trained teachers. More serious still, the sermon has changed its character. It no longer deals with doctrine, or at least so seldom as to be practically negligible, and for the gap thus made no adequate substitute has been provided. Whereas Protestantism began by teaching its laymen to understand the doctrines and principles of the Christian religion, while the Roman Church deliberately fostered their ignorance, today all this is reversed. It is the Roman Church which provides instruction in religion for its laymen. The Protestant Church leaves its members to pick up such knowledge as they can by themselves.

There are many reasons for this, into which we could enter at length if this were the time and place. The spirit of the age, with its demand for deeds, not words, is one reason. The pressure of other interests, robbing the minister of the quiet hours of study on which his predecessors could count, is another. Not least important, though largely unconfessed, is the lack of clear-cut and definite conviction which is the result of the radical changes introduced into men's beliefs by modern scholarship. All these influences and others besides have been at work and have produced changes in the attitude of the minister toward this most central and fundamental part of his task which are beginning to cause grave concern to thoughtful observers. Protestantism, I repeat, which might almost be defined as the religion of the teacher, has all but abandoned to Catholicism this most important of its functions.

If indeed we could rely upon our schools and colleges for furnishing the needed education, it would be different, but unlike Great Britain and the continental countries, we make no provision for the teaching of religion in our public schools. Indeed so fearful are we of sectarian teaching that so late as 1926 the Baptist General Association of Virginia addressed to the General Assembly a memorial opposing even the compulsory reading of the Bible in the public schools. No doubt there are reasons in our past history which make this attitude entirely explicable. The fact remains that great numbers of our children are growing up practically pagan with not even a bowing acquaintance with that greatest of all our treasures, not only as religion but as literature, the English Bible. And when we come to our colleges and universities the situation is little better. In the church-supported institutions religion is still a subject of instruction, but in the great Eastern colleges like Yale and Harvard, founded though they were for the primary purpose of providing a godly ministry, religion has been relegated to the position of an elective and in many of our great state universities it may not be taught at all.

How great then is the responsibility which is laid upon the minister to do what he can to overtake this lack! How serious in the light of all these facts becomes the comparative subordination of the teaching office in Protestantism.

It is true, thank God, that we are coming to realize the seriousness of our situation and to take measures to meet it. One of the most encouraging features of contempory religious life is the renewed emphasis laid in many quarters upon the importance of the teaching of religion. This appears in various ways: in the increased attention paid to the Sunday school, and the improvement of the helps provided for Sunday school teachers; in the provision in many seminaries for instruction in religious pedagogy and the psychology of religion; in the work of the Religious Education Association, and other similar agencies for bringing together men and women interested in the problems of religious education; in the free discussion of religious difficulties in the student conferences held under the auspices of the Christian Associations, and the improvement of the quality of the literature put forth by the Association presses. These are signs of a new and better day for which we have every reason to be grateful. But encouraging as they are they do not alter the fact that for the Church at large the situation is as I have described it and that the rank and file of ministers fail to take the teaching office seriously.

Indeed there is some danger that in our emphasis upon the more technical aspects of the teacher's work we may overlook the central and most important part of it—the content. As ministers of a historic religion we hold in trust a body of knowledge which it is our responsibility to transmit, enriched, if we may, by the confirmation of our experience, but in its substance unimpaired for the generations that come after us.

I make no apology, therefore, for the emphasis I lay on the teaching aspect of the minister's work. It may be difficult. It may be taxing. We may not succeed with it as

well as we hope. But no one can deny that it is important
—one might almost say, all important.

2. THE CHRISTIAN FACTS AS SUBJECT OF TEACHING

And first, of the subject matter of our teaching. What
are we, who are called to be teachers, to teach? I answer,
a very definite, but at the same time a many-sided and
elusive thing. We are to teach Christianity.

As Christian ministers, I repeat, we are to teach Christianity. That seems a very simple and obvious thing to
say, but the more we examine it the more questions it raises.
For our present purpose Christianity means at least three
different things. In the first place, it means a collection of
facts in history—a definite body of happenings that are
objectively given. In the second place, it means a gospel
—a message of deliverance and hope to the individual, a
program of redemption and transformation for society.
Finally, it means an institution, or rather a group of institutions, inwrought into the structure of our social life,
of which the particular church to which we belong is part.
All three of these aspects of Christianity the minister must
understand if he is to discharge his responsibility as a
teacher.

Expanding our first definition in the light of this analysis, we may rephrase it as follows: We are to teach the
story of the Christian religion, its message to the individual
and to society, and the nature and function of the institution through which it expresses itself in common action.

We are to teach the Christian religion. This gives definiteness to our work as teachers. There is a specific sub-

ject matter for the knowledge of which we are responsible, and this knowledge we are charged to share with others. This differentiates our work from that of other teachers with whom in many other respects we have much in common. It defines our subject matter in two ways: it takes some things in, and it leaves some things out.

It leaves some things out. As ministers we are not responsible for teaching everything. However free we may be to study and to teach whatever we like in the time which remains after our primary duty has been discharged, we are not responsible for teaching anything that lies outside our chosen field. There are a hundred subjects, useful, interesting, and important, of which, with entire self-respect, we may remain ignorant, or at least possess only that measure of knowledge that goes with the culture of a gentleman. Sociology, political economy, physical science, art, literature: these are fields fascinating in their attraction in which the more widely we wander the better. But they are not *our* fields. We are not responsible for teaching any of these things. Our subject is Christianity.

But it *is* Christianity. This at least we must know, whatever else we leave out. We are not free, as others might be, to choose a subject just because it interests us. Our theme is assigned. We are committed to it by our profession. As Christian ministers it is our business to understand the religion that we profess, and to be able to impart our knowledge to those who do not possess it. No mastery, however complete, of any other theme, however worthy, can serve as substitute for ignorance here.

First of all we must know Christianity as a historical religion, a body of facts objectively given.

It is no doubt true that as Christians we are ministers of a spiritual religion; but spirit in religion, as in all other phases of human life, never meets us disembodied. It is incarnate in persons who live and act, and struggle and aspire, and leave the record of their personality in history. It has been embodied in institutions, with laws and customs and traditions that call forth loyalty and reverence. It has passed through a history of change and growth as it has touched other influences, outward and inward, and acted upon and been reacted on by them. This history the minister must know and be able to teach.

He must know the origin of the Christian religion, that fascinating story of which our Bible gives us the record, of those epoch-making days which witnessed the first contacts of men with the founder of our religion—contacts which revealed to them the fact that a new and original influence was operating in the life of the world. He must know the setting in which these contacts took place, the inheritance which Christianity took over from Israel, the forms of thought and action which Greece and Rome had forged for its use, the permanent human needs to which it appealed and still appeals.

He must know what followed these first beginnings, tracing the history of Christianity through its many-sided development from the faith of a handful of obscure and despised Jews to the dominant religion of Western civilization. He must know the different forms which it has assumed, Oriental, Greek, Roman, Protestant. Above all, he must know what it is doing in the world today, not only in the particular form which is most congenial to him and in the particular communion with which he may chance to be identified, but as a great and many-sided factor in the world's life, affecting many races and nations and institutions.

I venture to think that in spite of all our seminary training there are items in this list on which we might not find it easy to pass an examination. On the beginnings of our religion we might stand a test. With the main outlines of church history we are no doubt most of us familiar. But when it comes to understanding Christianity as a present fact, how much do we really know? What do we know of the life of other churches than our own—the Roman Catholic Church, for example, or the Russian Orthodox Church, or the churches of the farther East? And yet these are churches that minister to more than half our fellow Christians. What do we know of the Roman Catholic Church in this country, its plans, its activities, the influence which it is exerting, the causes which explain its hold upon the multitude of its adherents? What do we know of the new Christian churches that are growing up in the mission field, the church of Japan, for instance, or that new national church of India which is beginning to rise above the horizon? Yet these are facts which lie within the direct scope of our responsibility as teachers, facts which it is our business to know and to impart.

It is important for us to know them, not for their own sake only, interesting and necessary as this knowledge is, but because of their bearing on a larger question, namely, that of the nature of the Christian religion. We call ourselves Christians, but the Christianity we profess is very different from that which is practiced by many of our fellow Christians. What is the relation between these varying forms? Are they all alike legitimate? Are they all alike Christian? If so, Christianity must be a much larger and more inclusive thing than our ordinary practice would lead men to suspect. What is there common to all these different forms of Christianity which makes them Christian? What new and original thing did Jesus bring into the world, and where, under the crust of ritual and dogma and prejudice with which it is so often and so sadly overlaid, is it to be found in the world today? These are questions which he only can answer who knows the Christian facts in the large, not of the past only, but of the present, not of the part merely, but of the whole.

3. THE CHRISTIAN GOSPEL AS SUBJECT OF TEACHING

But we must come to closer grips with our task. We are to teach not the nature only, but the message of the Christian religion. Christianity is not merely fact. It is gospel. It came into the world as a message of redemption to men in need. It professed to bring forgiveness for sin, comfort in sorrow, spiritual power for right living, the promise of a better social order for mankind. Its founder was Teacher, indeed, but he was more than Teacher. He was Messiah, the Christ who was to establish the Kingdom of God and be the agent of his saving work. To such a claim it was impossible to be indifferent. It was either true or false. One must be for Christ or against him.

So from the first Christianity has been a missionary religion. It has had a message to the hearts of men which it could not but preach. Its ministers have been witnesses, ambassadors, pleading with men to be reconciled with God that he might make of them new creatures in Christ Jesus.

It has had a message to the individual man, first of all a message of personal salvation. To men conscious of sin and imperfection, living narrow, incomplete, unsatisfied lives, it has brought its word of deliverance and renewal. To the deep needs of the human heart it has spoken, the need of guidance, the need of forgiveness, the need of comfort, the need of strength, the need of inward harmony and peace. In all these varying aspects of human experience it has shown itself the religion of adequacy and power. We have spoken of Christianity as a fact of history, but no one can understand it even as a fact who does not perceive that it is more than fact. It is revelation of things unseen; it is promise of greater and better things to be; it is creative activity in the realm of the Spirit.

One cannot emphasize this aspect of the Christian religion too strongly, for it is this which gives it its present significance for human life. If Christianity were simply a body of facts to be known, we could teach them in school and let it go at that. But Christianity, I repeat, is more than fact. It is a voice, proclaiming salvation, summoning to service. And for this another setting is necessary. The platform must become a pulpit, and the school give place to the Church.

Yet the minister, when he preaches the gospel, does not

therefore cease to be a teacher. For the gospel grows out of a definite philosophy of life and it is addressed to certain specific needs. That philosophy the minister must understand, and those needs he must know if he is to discharge his function aright.

This means that he must be a teacher of doctrine. For doctrine, when understood aright, is only another name for the way in which successive generations of Christians have formulated the answer of Christianity to the permanent needs of the human heart; the need of guidance, which finds its answer in revelation; the need of forgiveness, which finds its satisfaction in the Cross; the need of inward harmony and peace, which finds its answer in the living God who is at once righteousness and wisdom and love.

But above all, the need of inspiration and leadership which finds its answer in the Christ. For the offer of salvation, we must never forget, is only half the Christian message. Christianity is challenge as well as promise; summons to conflict as well as assurance of peace. It not only professes to make something new out of the individual man, it invites him to become a maker of that which is new in others.

This, I am sure, is what those who deserve the name of men really want: We want something big enough to do, and Christianity gives it. One of my students once wrote a book on the world's supreme need.[1] It is the need of a man's job, a job that is many-sided enough to enlist all one's powers and so vast that one can never come to the

[1] Du Bois, J. H., *The Christian Task* (New York, 1920).

end of it. Such a job Christianity gives us in the Kingdom of God. We are to be fellow workers with God in creating the new and better social order under the Master Workman, Jesus Christ. We are to build a home for the spirit of man. We are to build with and under and after Jesus Christ, using the materials and following the plans which God, our Father, has provided, and sustained by the food he furnishes. We are to remake the world after the pattern shown on the mount.

Is not this a man's job, the job we want and need? Well, it is our business as ministers to understand this job and to explain it to our fellow workmen to whom God's invitation comes. We are to know the message of Christianity, and this is the biggest and best part of the message, bigger even and better than the message of personal salvation, important and essential as that may be. We are to teach men what it means to be a Christian, what it means for our emotions, what it means for our beliefs, but above all what it means for our purposes. We are to be Christ's recruiting agents in his work of enlisting soldiers for his army of peaceful and constructive labor.

4. THE CHRISTIAN CHURCH AS SUBJECT OF TEACHING

Already we have passed from the individual to the social aspect of the Christian message. We are to teach Christianity, we have said, its message to the individual and to society. This introduces us to a difficult and, among Protestants, a much-neglected subject—namely, that of the nature and function of the Church.

Am I wrong in saying that of all phases of the minister's work as teacher, this is the one for which he ordinarily feels himself least responsible? With reference to every other phase of the Christian message he will own that he has a duty to perform. He will tell the story of the Christian origins; he may lecture on the heroes of the Christian faith or on the great landmarks of Christian history; he will have much to say of Christ's message to the individual, whether it be on the side of personal salvation or of social service. Indeed, if he be a modern man, social service will be constantly on his lips and the Kingdom of God the theme of his frequent preaching. But of the Church in its familiar, everyday form as the institution of religion, he will have little or nothing to say. When he refers to institutional religion it will be in a depreciatory way, as something which concerns high Anglicans and Roman Catholics, from which we more enlightened Protestants have long ago freed ourselves. As the minister of a spiritual religion the Church in which he believes is the company of Christian believers, the society of men and women who share Christ's ideals and are loyal to his purposes.

It is easy to understand how this state of things has come about. It is a natural reaction against the exaggerated institutionalism of the Roman Catholic Church. About the Church of the sixteenth century all sorts of superstitious and mistaken notions had gathered against which our fathers protested. It claimed to be the sole mediator of salvation. It demanded unquestioning obedience from all Christians. It denied to the individual believer the right of direct access to God. It identified the Christian ministry with a sacerdotal caste. It assigned to the Bishop of Rome a superhuman authority and dignity only rightfully to be given to Christ himself. It was right to protest against this extravagance. It was natural that this protest should extend further and include in its scope the whole range of institutional religion.

It was natural, but it was none the less unfortunate, for institutions are as essential to religion as to every other form of social life. Without institutions common action in any form is impossible. Religion is no exception. The remedy for a false conception of the Church is a true one.

Such a true conception of the Church we Protestants have failed to provide, and we are reaping the consequences of our failure in the form which is most disastrous to the ideals we cherish. In the name of the Kingdom we thought that we could ignore the Church, and we find that our neglect of the Church has for the rank and file of men carried the Kingdom with it.

For whether we realize it or not, the Church in the familiar sense of that word as the institution of religion is the form in which the ordinary man touches the Christian religion. He judges Christianity by what he sees the Church doing; and if the great social ideals of which we have been speaking are not intimately associated with what he sees Christians do when (as we say) they go to church they cease for him to have religious significance. They are matters with which, however important and interesting they may be for their own sake, Christianity, as he understands it, has nothing to do.

If, then, we wish to recover for the average man that

large and generous conception of the Christian religion which we believe to be the true one, we must recover our lost interest in institutional religion. We must restore the Christian Church in the true Protestant conception of it to the central place which it held in the religion of our Puritan forefathers, while at the same time we banish from the conception (and let me add as even more important, from the practice) of the Christian Church those remnants of the older Roman Catholic view which still cling to the Puritan conception and which render it for us untenable and misleading.

It is to the credit of our Episcopal and Lutheran fellow Christians that more than any other group of Protestants they have recognized this obligation and provided for it in their plans for ministerial education. One of the greatest obstacles in the present-day movement for Christian unity is that the ministers of other churches are not equally well furnished. They realize the weakness of institutional religion. They have not adequately recognized its strength. And so they are not at home with those in whose religious life the Church as the institution of religion holds the central place.

When I say that the Church is the institution of the Christian religion I do not forget that it is more than this. In its largest and most comprehensive meaning it is the Christian society, the company of men and women touched by the Spirit of Christ, through whom his purposes are to be realized in the world.

But this society, like all human societies, cannot function without organization. In this lies at once its strength and its weakness. Its weakness, for no institution, even one divinely sanctioned and endowed, as we believe the Church to be, can transmit the full content of spiritual revelation without modification or impairment. What God reveals in a moment of inspiration to one of his children can never be completely reproduced. There is something in every human experience that is original and incommunicable. When we try to pass it on we come into the realm of interpretation, and that means compromise. Institutions are at once the instrument and the record of this necessary but imperfect transition. The Christian Church is no exception. Claiming to be perfect and infallible, it has failed to be that which it might have been. Nay more, it has often failed to receive credit for what it has really been. To judge the Church rightly we must judge it for what it is, an institution like other institutions, subject to all the laws and limitations of institutional life, differing only (but in this supremely) in the uniqueness of its subject matter and the paramount interest of the issues with which it deals.

But with this weakness goes a corresponding strength. The individual dies, the institution lives on. What would otherwise be lost it preserves. Through ritual and custom, through literature and tradition, through sentiments of loyalty and reverence lovingly handed down from generation to generation, it creates a corporate consciousness as real, if different in kind, from the consciousness of the individual. The child of great men who have gone before, it becomes the mother of great men who come after. It is the nursery of faith, the home of the soul.

"I love Thy kingdom, Lord,
    The house of Thine abode,
The Church our blest Redeemer saved
    With His own precious blood."

These are not the words of a weak man nor of a lover of authority in religion. They come from an old Puritan who had tasted the joys of freedom and did not propose to give them up. But they express all the better for that what an institution may mean in the life of a man with social vision and social conscience.

The close connection between Church and Kingdom has been recognized from the first. In the Apostle Paul's terminology the words overlap. The Church, like the Kingdom, is a spiritual conception. It is the Kingdom so far as realized in the world. Later ages have reversed the procedure. Instead of identifying Church with Kingdom, they have identified Kingdom with Church. Thus to the Roman Catholic the Kingdom is only another name for the triumph of institutional Christianity, and our Puritan forefathers, in spite of their stalwart Protestantism, retained more than a little of the pride of this institutional consciousness. What President Dwight loves and in which he glories may be called indifferently Church or Kingdom. We are experiencing a reaction from this exaggerated identification. To us Church and Kingdom are so different that we are apt to overlook the vital connection between them. The Church is not the Kingdom, but it is the agent by which the Kingdom is to be established. It is the institution of the Christian religion, the social means by which the purposes of that religion are to be accomplished.

[178]

But this is true only within the limits which the definition itself sets. The Church is the agent for bringing in the Kingdom in the measure that it really is what it professes to be, the form in which the Christian religion finds social expression. Christianity, we have seen, is not merely fact, but revelation. It saves men by revealing God; it redeems society by bringing to bear upon every phase of human relationship the principles which God has revealed as determining the right relation between his creatures and himself. The Church establishes the Kingdom not by becoming the Kingdom, but by inspiring in men and women motives and ideals which, carried out through the appropriate agencies in all the relations of life, will bring the Kingdom to pass.

This is not prophecy merely. Where the Church has been what she ought to be, the expected results have followed. There is a story here which it is the minister's business to know and to tell. We call it the story of Christian missions. It is much larger and more inclusive than what goes technically by that name. It is the whole story of the expansion of Christianity through the creation of institutions which are self-perpetuating and self-reforming. It is a story which has become so familiar to us that we fail to realize its revolutionary significance or measure the possibilities of world promise that it contains. It is only when we open such a volume as that which has been prepared for us by that veteran of missions, Dr. Arthur J. Brown,[2] and contrast the group of facts there assembled with those that have formed our daily reading for the last

---

[2] *One Hundred Years* (New York, 1936).

dozen years as we have followed the tragic story of the aftermath of the Great War—it is only, I repeat, in the light of such a contrast that we appreciate what it means for the world that there should be such an institution as the Christian Church, committed in spite of all its imperfections to ideals of unselfish service, training its members in habits of systematic giving for people whom they have never seen, using for its daily and weekly textbook that unique record of man's aspirations and God's answer to them in redemptive experience which we call our Bible.

This whole subject of the missionary ideals and achievements of the Church is one that needs to be taught. It is the story of a great institution recreating itself in other institutions which in turn become the parents of new creative activity. To appreciate what it means you must have seen with your own eyes the contrast between Christian and non-Christian civilization. And yet how many people there are, otherwise benevolent and well-meaning, who still think of foreign missions as no proper concern of the American churches and who tell us that missions, like charity, begin at home.

If only they would act on their own words it would not be so bad. For here, too, there is a story to be told which needs telling. New forces are active in our home Christianity, a new ideal of what the Church means and what it should do. Where our fathers thought of home missions as carrying the gospel to the frontier and planting churches and Sunday schools in sparsely settled regions, we think of it as mobilizing all the spiritual resources of the Church for the task of Christianizing America. It is not New

Mexico and Wyoming alone which are home mission territory, but New York and Boston and Chicago; not Pole and Russian and Italian alone, but native Americans, the rich as well as the poor, the fortunate as well as the outcast and the destitute; not merely the laborer, but the man who employs him, and the banker who supplies the funds which keep the wheels of industry moving. This story, too, the story of the new home missions, the minister must know and be able to tell so that its full significance will be understood by his own people and for his own community.

5. SOME PRACTICAL DIFFICULTIES AND HOW TO MEET THEM

But I think I hear some one say, All that you have been telling us may be true so far as it goes, but it is irrelevant. What you have given us would serve as an excellent curriculum for a theological university, but how does it bear upon the work of us who are parish ministers, many of us in small communities with limited resources and little or no access to the books we need to fit us for such a task?

I realize the justice of such a criticism. It is true that what I have been giving you is an ideal that cannot be realized at once, and for many of us cannot be realized at all without outside help. But it is true of every ideal that is worth having that it exceeds our present power to realize. Enough if it sets a mark at which to aim.

But because the parish minister cannot realize that ideal immediately or without help it does not follow that there is nothing that he can do. One book at least he possesses which, if he uses it aright, will carry him a long way. And that is the Bible. With a good church history, an outline of Christian theology, a history of Christian missions, and a selection of the great liturgies he can make a start. And there ought to be made available to him through the authorities of the Church or through the college or seminary to which he belongs such other books as he may need for further study if only he has the will to use them.

I realize only too well that for the purpose I have in mind the opportunities which are open to the minister of a small parish along this line are woefully inadequate. But because that is so now there is no reason why it should continue to remain so. If enough ministers make up their minds to take their teaching function seriously, it will not be beyond the power of the Church to which they belong to furnish them the help they need.

But more important than access to any particular book or books is the insight that will enable the minister to use what he reads aright. And here his own experience must, under God, be his teacher.

For this work of the minister as teacher differs from that of many other teachers in that it is conditioned at all points by a definite practical aim. We ministers are first of all evangelists, and that means missionaries. Our appeal is to the will. As Paul put it long ago, "We are ambassadors for Christ, as though God did beseech you by us: be ye reconciled to God." [3] It is just because such momentous practical issues hang upon the decisions to which we invite men that we cannot afford to make mistakes as to the facts. When we appeal, as we must, to the experience of

[3] 2 Corinthians 5: 20.

those who have tried Christ's way before us, it is essential that we should be able to give chapter and verse to what we say.

This combination of a practical aim with a scrupulous regard for the facts is a mark of every great teacher. More and more our modern teachers are coming to realize that above and beyond their responsibility as transmitters of knowledge they have a further and higher responsibility as formers of character. But what in their case is incidental to their main task is primary in the work of the minister. It is his privilege to see God at work in his world and to pass on to all whom he can reach the insight he has attained, that they, looking where he has looked, may see what he has seen and act accordingly.

How this aim is to be realized in detail will be our concern in the chapters that follow. But there is one suggestion that comes to us from modern educational theory that requires brief consideration in these closing words.

6. HOW THE NEEDS OF THE PUPILS DETERMINE THE METHOD OF THE TEACHER

All teaching that is to be effective, we are told, however objective it may be in content, must, if it is to accomplish its purpose, be relevant to the capacity and needs of the pupil. If this be true of teaching in general, how much more must it be true of the minister's teaching.

Whom, then, is the minister to teach? The answer can be given in a sentence. First of all his own congregation, and after that all the other people he can reach.

I say, first of all his own congregation. This is a most

[183]

important point on which we cannot insist too strongly at the outset. The minister is not free to choose whom he shall teach any more than he is free to choose what he shall teach. He has a definite responsibility given him for a particular group of people. They are his point of contact with the larger world of men. What he does he must do through them. What he knows he must impart to them. Whatever may be true of others, for him success or failure must be judged by what happens in the minds of the men and women and children into whose faces he looks from Sunday to Sunday.

At first sight this seems a disheartening limitation, for the average parish is not, for the superficial observer, the most exciting field for the display of a mature man's intellectual powers. Many people still think of the parish minister primarily as a consoler of old ladies and a planner of Sunday school picnics. And you know only too well by your own experience how much routine enters into the minister's life; how easy it is to lower one's ideal to the measure, I will not say of the actual, but of the immediately visible; how remote from the interests that fill the lives of the men and women you touch from week to week in your congregations seem the profound and complicated questions which we passed in review when we tried to define the subject matter of the minister's teaching.

It may help to reconcile us somewhat to the situation to remember that some such limitation is inherent in the task of every teacher. The teacher who is really effective is never a teacher of people in general. He is always the teacher of something to somebody. Numerous as his pupils may be, remote as may seem his opportunities of personal contact, he is always touching individuals with some specific thought which is meant for them. He is not concerned with truth in general, the abstract principles and general laws of which the man of science is in quest, but with truth in its application to the needs and aspirations of some particular human being or group of human beings.

There is limitation in this, but there is compensation, too, for it gives concentration and definiteness to effort. The teacher touches life at first hand. He is a doer. Teaching is personal communion, contact of spirit with spirit, creation in the realm where creation means most and carries farthest.

But we must bring the matter closer home. The minister, I say, is to teach his congregation, but who and what are the people who make up this congregation? When we look at them more closely we may be tempted to revise our earlier estimate, for they are not one, but many things, and each of the many things they are makes its own separate and unique appeal to the minister as teacher.

In the first place, a congregation is a group of individuals, each with his own separate and irreproducible life, who are growing up to Christian discipleship.

In the second place, a congregation is a collection of personalities living their lives under the conditions of time and space, but destined for immortality.

In the third place, a congregation is a body of Christians living in a definite locality who are responsible for the Christianization of their community.

In the fourth place, a congregation is a part of the one

undivided Church of Christ, and as such responsible with its fellow Christians of other congregations for the establishment of the Kingdom of God on earth.

Finally, a congregation is a cross section of humanity including men and women of many different tastes and occupations, and touching directly or potentially every major interest of mankind.

Here surely is a school big enough for any man's best efforts. A school, did I say? Rather should I have said a whole collection of schools, each with its own particular need and appeal, each presenting a fresh point of contact with the particular group of facts and truths which form the subject matter of the minister's teaching. All that this means for the minister's work we shall consider more in detail in the chapters that follow.

CHAPTER VIII

THE MINISTER AS PASTOR. TRAINING FOR CHRISTIAN LIVING

1. THE MINISTER AS COUNSELOR IN THE PROBLEMS OF APPLIED CHRISTIANITY

2. PRINCIPLES WHICH SHOULD GOVERN THE MINISTER IN HIS COUNSELING

3. HOW THE CHURCH CAN HELP THE MINISTER IN THE APPLICATION OF THESE PRINCIPLES

4. THE CHRISTIAN ATTITUDE TOWARD WAR AS AN EXAMPLE

5. SOME THINGS THE INDIVIDUAL MINISTER CAN DO

1. THE MINISTER AS COUNSELOR IN THE PROBLEMS OF APPLIED CHRISTIANITY

We saw in an earlier chapter that prayer is never a pure dialogue. It is not simply a conversation between God and the soul, though it is this. There is a third party to the conversation, present to thought even if not vocal—the brother for whom Christ gave his life. Where this social reference is absent we may have prayer indeed, but it is not Christian prayer.

This social reference was brought before me vividly in a conversation I had with a young Roman Catholic whom I met in Rome. We had been speaking of one of the most recent of the Roman Catholic saints, the young Carmelite, St. Thérèse of Lisieux, whom it has become the custom to call the "Little Flower."

St. Thérèse, it will be remembered, took the veil at an exceptionally early age, and after a life of extreme privation died at an age when most of our young people are just entering upon their life work.

One of my friends, a lady of earnest Christian character, had criticized the authorities of the Convent for the austerities which they allowed this fragile young creature to undergo. There seemed to her something unnatural, almost revolting, in the life of solitude to which the Carmelite vow condemned her. "Ah!" said the young Catholic to whom she was speaking, "you do not understand. It was her desire to suffer *for us.*"

This social reference, present even in the most austere and (as it often seems to us Protestants) unnatural forms of Catholic piety, distinguishes our Christian gospel from all purely mystical faiths. There are three, I repeat, concerned in Christian prayer: God, the self, and the brother. As the Godward reference distinguishes our Christian gospel from Humanism in all its forms, so the social reference distinguishes it from all forms of purely introspective and individualistic religion. We go into our closet and shut the door that we may be alone with God, and we find that the brother whom we thought we had shut out is there before us in the loving purpose of him whom Jesus has taught us to call our Father.

This discovery forms a natural point of transition to a further aspect of the minister's work, that of personal counselor in the many-sided problems that are involved in the application of religion to daily life. The minister, as our Protestant fathers conceived his office, is not simply a prophet, bringing men a message from God concerning his purpose for mankind. He is not simply a priest, helping them to realize their personal relation to God as a present fact—more than this, as the fact of facts. He is a pastor, helping them to draw the practical consequences which follow from this fact for their own lives and for the life of society. This, in our confused and troubled world, is far from easy.

It is not easy, even in connection with the more personal aspects of Christian living, the formation of right habits through the discipline of the emotions, the cultivation of humility and of thankfulness, the banishing of fear, through the practice of the presence of God. Those who have taken the pastoral office most seriously know best how much the average man and woman needs help in this most intimate field.[1]

But character is not formed in a vacuum. It develops through relationships; and these relationships confront the Christian who would take his social responsibility seriously with a host of problems on which he has a right to look to his minister for help.

This conception of the minister's work as practical counselor in the problems of applied Christianity is rooted, as all conceptions of the minister's function must be, in the Christian experience of God. There are views of religion in which the minister's responsibility has been fully discharged when he has provided a point of contact between the soul and God by the celebration of the public ritual of religion. It is not so in Christianity. The God we worship is ethical personality. He has revealed himself in Jesus Christ, not only as righteous and loving, but as summoning his worshipers to share his life of righteousness and love. They are to be holy as he is holy. And holiness in the

---

[1] In Chapter V (pp. 131-135) I have made some suggestions as to ways in which this help can be given.

[191]

Christian conception of it is not a life wholly detached from the world in mystic contemplation, but a life of active service in which the redeemed soul expresses its gratitude to God for his forgiveness by carrying into all the relationships of life that same spirit of compassionate goodwill of which our Lord and Saviour Jesus Christ has given us the first and great example.

When life was simpler than it is today, the duty of service was conceived largely in terms of individual helpfulness. It meant feeding the hungry, clothing the naked, housing the homeless, healing the sick, visiting the prisoners. And this is still a part of our Christian duty. But today we see that hunger and sickness, destitution and crime, are effects of preceding causes, many of them of highly involved and technical character. And when we analyze these causes to find who is responsible for them, we discover that that responsibility is often carried home to our own door. These social evils which bear their fruit in individual suffering and sorrow are by-products of a social system in which we are all involved and to which we are all contributors. So little by little our ideal of service has been expanding until it takes in cause as well as effect. We are responsible, so we believe, not simply for healing the wounds that social maladjustment has caused but for changing the system which makes these wounds inevitable.

This was the new insight which came a generation ago to men like Walter Rauschenbusch and which gave impetus to what we often call the Social Gospel. The Social Gospel is only our way of saying that what Christianity contemplates is not only the redemption of individuals out of the world, but the redemption of the world itself.

This conception of the social implications of the gospel not only sets the minister his task but presents him with his problem. For while all Christians agree that it is God's purpose ultimately to redeem society as well as all individuals in it, not all agree as to the time and way in which this is to be done. Some Christians, as we have seen, despair of any social redemption during the course of human history, and therefore postpone to the life to come the establishment of the new social order. Others look for the Kingdom of God on this earth to be sure, but as a result of a miraculous transformation to be brought about instantaneously at the second coming of our Lord. Still others believe not only that social salvation is possible during our own lifetime, but that they themselves know the way in which it is to be brought about, while very many Protestants hold an intermediate position. They accept the social interpretation of the gospel as committing them to dealing with the causes of social evil as well as its effects. But when they are asked what follows for their own duty, they are honestly perplexed. If only one could live in one of the two worlds at a time, the world of business and politics, where competition is the law and the prizes of success go to the strongest and the cleverest, or the world of religion, where love is the law, and he is greatest who is servant of all, one's duty would be comparatively easy. But the Christian, as we have seen, is citizen of both these worlds, and it is his function to live in the secular world as becomes a son of God and a disciple of Jesus Christ. What can the minister do to help him here?

2. PRINCIPLES WHICH SHOULD GOVERN THE MINISTER IN HIS COUNSELING

There is no phase of the minister's work, you will agree with me, that presents greater difficulties, for the problems with which he is called to deal not only concern aspects of life of which he often lacks firsthand knowledge, but aspects of life in which change is so rapid that even when he thinks he knows his knowledge becomes out of date almost as soon as it is acquired.

Some years ago it was my privilege to take part in a study of theological education, and one of the questions we asked the graduates of our seminaries was, "What were the subjects in which you believe your seminary training was most conspicuously deficient?" There was general agreement that among these the training given for the pastoral office was most disappointing. Again and again we met the complaint that when the graduates of our seminaries met their parishioners in the daily work of the parish they were faced by problems with which their seminary training had not fitted them to cope.

As a seminary teacher for many years I must confess that the criticism is justified. But I must add that the theological teacher is not the only one to blame. He reflects the uncertainty that we find in the Church as its leaders try to feel their way through the complicated process of social readjustment in which we find ourselves involved.

Clearly we face problems here with which the individual

is helpless to cope unaided. Take, for example, the question of war and peace. There is no subject on which we find deeper and more widespread conviction among Christians than that it is our business to put an end to war. Yet when we attempt to frame a definite program for action, we find convictions differing. Shall we attempt to commit the Church to the absolute pacifist position, or must we distinguish between aggressive and defensive war? If we take the latter position, what are the tests by which aggression must be determined? When war arises between other nations, what ought the attitude of our country to be? Must we maintain neutrality at all hazards, even if this means denying to a nation attacked access to materials necessary to its own defense? Are we to be neutral, not simply in act but in thought, taking no account of the considerations of justice which may enter into the conflict? The more one faces these questions seriously, the more one perceives how many factors enter into them, how difficult it is to give a ready-made solution which shall do justice to all the facts of the case.

What is true of war and peace is true to greater or less extent of all the social questions on which the Christian must take a position, questions of the ethics of business, the respective rights of capital and labor, the best way of dealing with divorce, etc. In all these questions we find sincere Christians honestly differing, yet it is on these questions that the minister is called upon to give his advice.

What then is the minister to do when he finds difficulties of this kind? One thing that he can do is to seek counsel from those who have had more experience than himself.

I shall have something to say in a moment as to the sources from which such counsel may be had. But advice as to matters of detail will avail him little unless he has a clear conception of the purpose which should control all the Christian's activity and the way in which, in spite of the limitations of his knowledge, one Christian may help another in their application.

First of all then the minister must hold constantly before his eyes the ideal of brotherly love to which Jesus Christ has committed us in the gospel. And wherever he may find in the life of the community of which he is a part any departure from this ideal, he must call attention to it and lay upon the conscience of his people the duty of finding a way to remedy it. He may not himself know what that remedy is; he may not be able to point out the exact steps through which it is to be reached. That does not relieve him of the responsibility of holding constantly before men's eyes the contrast between their present conduct and the divine ideal.

In the next place the minister must familiarize himself, so far as it is possible for him to do so, with the experience of the men who have faced similar problems and difficulties before him, so that whatever their experience may have to teach may be made available to his own people. I feel sure that it is at this point that our present practice has been most at fault. There is a body of evidence available as to the ways in which the application of Christian principles has led to the solution or at least to the great amelioration of social difficulties. With this evidence it should be the minister's duty to familiarize himself, so that he may be able to pass it on to those who may find it suggestive in their own case. But it is not easy, for many of us it is impossible without help from others, to gain access to it. No more useful service could be rendered by those who are responsible for the leadership of the Church than to bring together in a form convenient for use by the parish minister the most helpful illustrations of the past experience of the Church in ways of dealing successfully with social difficulties.

More important still is it for the minister to insist that in any approach to controversial matters on which people feel deeply it is the spirit that matters most. When the right spirit is lacking there is no recourse but to force, and solutions reached by force alone are never lasting solutions. If demonstration of this were needed, the conclusion of the last war would have given it in convincing degree. But the principles which apply to the strife of nations apply in equal measure to social controversy in every form. If you wish to reach a right solution of any matter in which you are in controversy with your neighbor, you must first convince him that you think of him as a human being with equal rights and interests with your own, with whom you desire to enter into amicable relations by every possible means. Where such a spirit obtains agreement may not at once be reached, but the worst danger of disagreement will be avoided. Fellowship will remain unbroken in spite of difference and, for the Christian, fellowship is the thing that matters most.

One thing more we have a right to expect of the minister, and that is that he shall maintain in spite of every discouragement an unconquerable faith in the applicability of the principles of Christ to every phase of our social life.

In recent years there has grown up a literature which, while admitting that in the field of individual ethics the law of reason and of love is applicable, is inclined to be skeptical as to the power of reason and love to solve the problems of society. Man, the individual, these writers hold, is, or may become, moral, but the limitations to which men's action in society is subject make that action too often immoral (or at least unmoral). For the solution of our social problems, therefore, there seems to remain no recourse but force.[2]

If this be so, it is a gloomy outlook indeed, for what force alone can do to bring peace into our troubled world we see drastically illustrated by what has happened in the Great War and what is even now happening in Spain. Let it be granted that to the human eye there seems no way to reach a practicable solution. It is the business of the man of faith to fix his eyes upon the unseen Actor to whom all things are possible, and never to lose his confidence that in the end his purpose will prevail.

We touch here the basic issue of our Christian faith, the question of God's presence in history. If we have been right in affirming that presence, then, dark as the present outlook may seem, the future is secure. If, on the other hand, this faith of ours be vain, then we have no recourse but the law of the jungle.

This, then, is the duty of the minister in the matter of

[2] Professor Reinhold Niebuhr is commonly credited with holding this view, but Professor John Coleman Bennett, in the Spring Number of *Religion in Life*, 1937, has shown that this is true only with qualifications.

applying Christian principles to social life: first, to keep ever before the eyes of men the ideal of brotherhood to which Christ has committed us; secondly, to learn what the past experience of other Christians has to teach us of the way in which in the past love has found its way to the right solution of difficult social problems; thirdly, to keep a quiet and loving spirit in spite of every temptation to passion and bitterness; and finally, never to lose faith in the ultimate triumph of the good.

3. HOW THE CHURCH CAN HELP THE MINISTER IN THE APPLICATION OF THESE PRINCIPLES

But, I think I hear some one say, all this may be true as far as it goes. We accept your statement of the principles that should govern our approach to social problems. We have been trying as far as knowledge and strength will permit to apply them to the situation in which we find ourselves, but there are so few who feel as we do and we can do so little alone. Is there not something more that you can say than you have said? Has not the Church in its organized capacity a larger responsibility to help its ministers than it has thus far been willing to assume?

I believe that it has. But for us Protestants that responsibility must be met in a Protestant way—that is, by the way of common study and experiment. In the Church of Rome the priest may receive definite instructions as to the advice he must give in the confessional. Any counsel we may give must come with the free consent both of adviser and advised.

This does not mean, however, that there is no help that

we can give one another, only that we must mobilize our resources for use. There are stores of experience laid up for us in the history of the Church and in the lives of great Christians which could be of the greatest assistance to us in dealing with our practical problems today. It is the responsibility of the Church in its organized capacity to gather this information and to make it available for us in convenient and easily accessible form. But this cannot be done without more extended co-operation than we have yet achieved.

It is encouraging, therefore, that our Protestant churches are beginning to recognize their corporate responsibility in such matters and are organizing studies designed to clarify thought and suggest methods of procedure. The study of *Church and State in Contemporary America,* already referred to, is an example of such co-operative study, and the studies which have been carried on in preparation for the recent Conference at Oxford on "Church, Community, and State" have done much to clarify our thinking on points of difficulty.

But it is not enough that there should be occasional studies dealing with special aspects of our perplexing social problems. What we need is a group of students who are functioning all of the time and for us all. A modest beginning has been made in the Department of Research and Education of the Federal Council. A parallel in the international field is the Research Department of the Universal Christian Council for Life and Work. It is to the studies of the latter that I owe my information about the spread of the atheistic movement in Russia, and it is this department which was charged with the organization of the co-operative studies that prepared the way for the Oxford Conference.

All this is good as far as it goes. But what we Protestants are doing together seems child's play compared with what the Roman Catholics are doing. Our Research Department in the United States commands the services of two full-time and two part-time research workers. The Universal Christian Council has two full-time workers. The corresponding organization of the Roman Catholics, The Action Populaire, of Paris, commands the services of nineteen full-time fathers. Is it any wonder that to our Roman Catholic friends we Protestants, in spite of all our talk about the Social Gospel, seem only half in earnest?

There are two limitations which their present organization and program impose upon the existing research agencies of the Protestant churches. They can deal only with the points of most acute controversy, and this usually only when issues have been joined which make a peaceable solution difficult. Moreover, even in the case of those controversies with which they deal they must for the most part confine their work to an objective analysis of the issues presented, leaving to others the story of the constructive measures by which other Christians have dealt successfully with similar cases. In other words, to use a medical analogy, they conceive their work as one of diagnosis rather than of therapy, and leave the more fruitful field of preventive medicine largely uncultivated.

Let us take, for example, the work of the Research Department of the Federal Council. When one considers the limitations under which this department operates, the wonder is not that it has done so little, but that it has done so much. During the thirteen years of its existence it has made no less than a dozen studies of controverted social issues in the field of applied Christianity. Among these studies are those of prohibition, of the Mexican-American Oil and Land Controversy, of the Western Maryland strike, of the Centralia riots, of the motion picture industry, of the chaplaincy, and more recently of the relation of church and state in contemporary America. On all these subjects it has assembled data not otherwise easily accessible, has analyzed the issues at stake, pointing out the moral and religious factors involved. It has presented the views of the different parties to the controversy, with the arguments on either side, and so put those on whom the responsibility for ultimate decision must rest in the possession of the material which would make a just judgment possible. In addition it has maintained an Information Service, in which it has dealt in a similar objective manner with such items of the current news as involved moral issues or presented moral problems.

This is a service of high value, for which we can only be thankful. It is a cause for gratitude that when controversy arises the Church possesses an agency on which it can rely for impartial study and unprejudiced report.

But one covets for the Church an agency which, while doing all that the Research Department now does, shall add to its present function of analysis that of corporate witness. When controversy reaches the acute stage at which it ordinarily becomes the concern of the department it is often too late to apply the needed remedy. Prestige is involved, and passion has been kindled, and even when the Christian way of solution is clearly seen it is not easy to persuade those upon whom the final decision must rest to use it.

Surely we have another and a greater responsibility than this—namely, that of setting in motion the forces that will make possible the right solution of difficult social questions before it is too late. If we have been right in our account of the Christian gospel, it is the gospel of a God who is at work in his world, not only judging, but redeeming. What we have to bring men is not simply an ideal, important and indeed essential as that is, but evidence that there is a power at work in the world which is translating that ideal into reality. That is what we mean by saying that the supreme function of the minister is that of evangelist, a bringer of the good news that God is actually at work in his world. But the evidence of that fact is the transformation that faith in him has produced and is producing in the lives of individuals and of society.

We have long recognized this in the case of the individual. The successful evangelists have made witness their stock in trade. Their message to those whom they would win to the gospel has been that of the blind man in the Fourth Gospel: "Whereas I was blind, now I see." [3] They have had a story to tell of changed lives, and to men who met their message with a denial of its possibility they have had their answer ready: "With men this is impossible; but with God all things are possible." [4]

[3] John 9: 25.   [4] Matthew 19: 26.

It is not otherwise with the Social Gospel. Evangelism, whether in the case of the individual or of society, is in the last analysis witness. It is the story of what God has done and is doing, and the evidence of his doing is the transformation of human life which has taken place.

The difficulty is that no one of us alone commands the evidence by which this assertion is to be justified. Social change takes place slowly and can only be rightly judged in the perspective of the years. Even when part of the evidence is in our possession it often fails to carry conviction because it is not put into relation to other data of which we have no knowledge.

During my attendance at the Ministers' Conference at Dallas it was my privilege to take part in an open forum which was conducted by one of the speakers. He began by asking every one who was present to give his testimony as to social evils which had come under his notice in his capacity as minister. Half an hour was spent in a survey of this kind, and enough evidence was gathered to justify the most discouraging conclusions of our contemporary pessimists. Then the leader suggested that it might be well to change the emphasis and requested those who had encouraging features of the social situation to report to give their testimony. The time that remained proved too short to hear all those who had such testimony to give, but enough was said to make it evident that side by side with the discouraging factors in contemporary life there were things happening all along the line which showed that Christ's Spirit was functioning even in those aspects of our social relationship, such as race, economic relations, and

Christian co-operation, where, apart from such testimony, discouragement would have been easy. While each item taken alone might seem of slight importance, the impression made by the whole was heartening.

What these Texan ministers were able to do by the sharing of their experiences suggests what might be done by a similar procedure on a nation-wide—or better still, on a world-wide—scale. Here would seem to be a field which could wisely be cultivated by some agency like the Research Department if it made it its task to assemble the available evidence of the way in which Christ's Spirit has been functioning in the social field during the last generation and to point out the aspects of this functioning which might prove suggestive to persons facing similar problems in our own day.

Take the field of race relations, surely, in face of what is happening in the world today, one of the most difficult and baffling of all the fields for the application of Christian principles. And yet if we contrast the present situation in our country with that which met us a decade, not to say a generation, ago, we find much to justify hope. In the South, where hitherto the race question has been most acute, a new consciousness is awake. It shows itself not only in the growing condemnation of lynching, taking the form even in some cases of willingness to accept a federal law for dealing with the evil, but more particularly in the fact that in our colleges there is a growing disposition to face the question of race seriously and to work out by experiment more helpful types of relationship. Especially impressive is the growing conviction that if any solution of the race question is to be found, it must be through the education of the backward members of both races.

More than forty-five years ago a little group of Northerners started a school for Negroes in the Black Belt of Alabama. Their presence was looked on askance by many of their neighbors, and they were forced to rely for their chief support upon help from outside. But they were not discouraged, and little by little won their way to the confidence of their neighbors.

A few weeks ago that school was visited by a delegation of Southern friends, including the editor of a leading journal. They were so much impressed by what they saw that they determined to give their impressions the widest possible publicity. So a careful article was prepared about what was being done and attention was called to it in a leading editorial under the caption "Introduction to Living," in which the work of the school was held up to Southern people as a profound contribution to the solution of the "delicate and difficult problem of racial relations." [5]

Or take the scarcely less perplexing field of economic relationships. On the face of it, it seems as if, far from making progress, we were facing problems more acute than in any other generation. But this is due largely to the fact that our standards have been changing. Conditions which would have been taken for granted as inevitable a generation ago now seem to us intolerable. And while on the national, and still more on the international, scale we still seem far from finding the solution we need, experiments

[5] *Birmingham Age-Herald,* January 19, 1937.

are being tried which are full of suggestion for the future. It is in Japan, most imperialistic of nations, that Kagawa has been working out his experiments in economic co-operation; while Sweden, that most progressive of European countries, is showing us that it is possible, if the will be there, to combine many of the advantages of capitalism and socialism. In the field of the relations of capital and labor, hitherto one of the most baffling of all the problems in the contemporary scene, experiments are being tried that are full of promise for the future.

I am not attempting to pass any judgment as to the truth of the different estimates of our present social situation made by our contemporary optimists and pessimists. All that I am saying is that before we pass judgment we need to assemble all the available information, and that among this information that which is afforded by the efforts to apply Christian principles to the solution of social problems is most relevant. Here at least is a place at which help can be brought to those discouraged parish ministers who are trying in isolation to deal with social situations with which they feel themselves unable alone to cope.

4. THE CHRISTIAN ATTITUDE TOWARD WAR AS AN EXAMPLE

It is against the background of such experiences that we must approach the most baffling of all the social issues which confront us today, the question of the Christian attitude toward war. Nowhere is it more necessary to take a long look and to see things in their larger perspective.

The first fact that meets us when we approach this problem is that it is universally recognized as a problem. This is something new under the sun. That war was a recognized way of settling national disputes was with a few rare exceptions generally admitted. It was the assumption of the Christian creeds and the theme of many of the liturgies. But today we recognize that war is evil and that it is the Church's duty to work to realize a warless world. That of itself is a great step forward and must be recognized as our first ground of hope.

But when we ask how this end is to be accomplished we meet the fact that there exist honest differences of conviction among Christians. Some, as we have seen, holding an absolutist philosophy, believe war in every form to be an evil in which the Christian should have no part, and so accept the position of consistent pacifism. Others recognize that in our imperfect political and economic system there are tensions for which up to the present time no other outcome than war has yet been found. They find a way out by distinguishing between offensive and defensive war and confining the Christian's duty to the latter. Here we seem to be in a field in which the individual minister is in an almost hopeless position and where, if ever, he has a right to call upon the central authorities of the Church for help.

As an example of the kind of help such co-operative approach can give the parish minister, let me cite a list of propositions which are to be found in the recent study of *Church and State in Contemporary America*.[6] These propositions deal with the vexed question of the Christian's duty

[6] *Op. cit.*, pp. 275-278.

in time of war. Their purpose is to outline a platform on which, in spite of the serious differences which still separate them, the leaders of the different churches may unite. This platform includes the following planks:

"1. The Church should make clear that the method of settling political controversies by war is wrong in principle and, however laudable may be its purpose in any particular case, has by-products which in the long run must mean disaster for all concerned. If admitted at all, it must always be as the lesser of two evils.

"2. When, as in the case of the Friends, conscience prevents the Christian from taking part in war in any form, either offensive or defensive, the Church should defend his right to exemption from military service, and should advocate the provision of alternative forms of service, which do not involve the taking of life. Should the conscientious objector refuse such service, the Church should seek to secure for him the considerate treatment which it is the duty of a humane state to give to offenders against its laws.

"3. When war has been entered into on grounds of national advantage or before every possible means of settlement by arbitration or by conciliation has been exhausted, it is the duty of Christians both individually and in their corporate capacity to register their protest. What form that protest will take, whether the direct refusal of military service by individuals or some form of corporate action, must be determined in the light of the particular situation.

"4. When war has been entered upon, for reasons which

appear to those citizens who are Christians as right (e.g., in self-defense or in support of a nation attacked by another nation declared an aggressor by a responsible international tribunal of which the nation concerned has been a part), the Christian who takes part in it should always remember that those against whom he fights are his brothers and should retain toward them the respect which becomes those who honestly differ as to their duty. If, in the madness which battle engenders, he for the moment forget this and feel and act toward them as enemies to be hated or obstacles to be destroyed, he should use the moments of returning sanity to repent of the sin in which, in spite of himself, he has been made to share, and to resolve, when war is over, to do his part in removing the causes which in our unbrotherly society now make war the final arbiter of national disputes.

"5. When war is over there should be complete forgiveness and peace should be concluded on terms which take full and even generous account of the interests of the conquered as well as of the victors.

"6. So long as the churches admit that a Christian may serve in the army and the navy, it is clearly their duty to provide for the religious needs of the soldiers and sailors. That provision is now made through chaplains appointed and paid by the government, the candidates for the position being recommended by a committee representing the churches. This arrangement is criticized by many, partly on the ground that the reception of pay from the government unduly limits the chaplain's freedom, partly that his status as an army or naval officer commits him to the sup port of existing military policy. Up to the present time, however, no satisfactory substitute for the chaplaincy has been found. Under these conditions it would appear that those who represent the churches have a double duty: that of helping the chaplains to render the best service they can under their present limitations; and at the same time of working to secure conditions more conducive to the full freedom of those who minister in the name of the Church to the soldiers and sailors.

"7. Above all, while peace still remains, it is the duty of the Church to urge upon every country that it should join with others not only in providing means for the settlement of international disputes which may otherwise lead to war, but in removing the political and economic causes which give rise to war and in working for the type of international organization which makes this possible. Where grievances exist under existing international law, it is the duty of the stronger nations to remove them by sharing their superior resources with the weaker, and where this involves changes in existing legislation (e.g., in the case of boundaries, the free exchange of raw materials, immigration, finance, or tariffs) it should be the duty of the Christian to work for this change.

"Here, again, it is not the responsibility of the Church to determine what the existing agency of change shall be, whether the existing League of Nations or a reconstituted League on different and more comprehensive lines. But it is the duty of the Church to insist that no nation live to itself alone and that for nations, as for individuals, the law holds that those who are strong ought to bear the infirmities of the weak and not to please themselves.

"More important than any specific position which the Church may take in time of war or in those still more momentous days when the issue between peace and war still hangs in the balance is its ceaseless reminder, in season and out of season, of the unity of mankind. Whether the League of Nations succeeds or fails in realizing its ideal of a universal society in the political field, the Church of Jesus Christ can never surrender its witness to a brotherhood which transcends nation and race. In its ideal, even if not as yet in outward manifestation, the Church is one. To make this unity apparent is the manifest duty of the churches."

5. SOME THINGS THE INDIVIDUAL MINISTER CAN DO

Whether this analysis of the principles which should determine the Christian's attitude toward war seems convincing or not, it will at least serve to call attention to one distinction of major importance—namely, the difference between the problem presented to the Christian conscience when war has actually broken out and that which meets us during the preceding period when the forces that make for peace and for war, respectively, are still striving for the mastery.

We may illustrate this difference in connection with a matter which is much in the public attention at the present time, the matter of neutrality. It may well be that when war has broken out between other nations, the wisest and the most helpful thing that any nation can do will be to reduce the area of conflict by taking whatever steps are necessary to preserve its own neutrality. But however wise and even necessary such a policy may be from the point of view of expediency, from the point of view of practical effectiveness and of Christian principle it leaves much to be desired.

And this for two reasons. In the first place, because the relations between the different peoples have become so intimate that any severance of relation so drastic as that involved in a policy of complete neutrality will involve so far-reaching a dislocation of normal relationships as to put a strain upon the national self-control which, as in the case of the last war, it may prove impossible permanently to resist. But in the second place, and more important, because it belongs to the very nature of the Christian religion to feel that what happens to other human beings is the concern of Christians everywhere. A policy of neutrality which ignores the moral issues involved in war and feels no responsibility to help those who may have been unjustly attacked does violence to deep convictions which grow out of the very nature of the Christian faith. Neutrality, therefore, can at most be regarded as a second best, the least harmful makeshift in a situation in which the true way out has already been missed.

The distinction thus made between the conditions presented by the existence of a social evil and that which obtains before the causes which produce it have reached the point of crisis is equally applicable to those less dramatic, but no less perplexing issues which meet us in connection with other phases of our social life, issues of race, of industry, of finance, and of commerce. The time to deal with an evil is before it is here. And the way to deal with it is to foster those influences of understanding and good will which, before passion has been aroused and prestige invoked, make a just and brotherly solution possible.

For the influences which make for war between nations, it cannot too often or too forcibly be said, are the same influences which make for strife in families and in communities: ignorance, selfishness, pride, fear—the very influences with which in their deepest roots Christianity, and Christianity alone, is able to deal.

For this reason the very limitations that often seem to baffle the minister when he is faced with the major problems of industrial strife or of war have their reverse side in the more intimate contacts which his work in the parish makes possible with the men and women who are the raw material of which nations and parties are made. When he is working for understanding and good will in the limited field which is his primary responsibility, he is doing more than the humdrum work of a parish minister. He is strengthening those forces of understanding and good will out of which alone enduring peace, whether in the nation or in the world, can be secured.

Here surely is a field where the minister's official position gives him exceptional opportunity of helpful service. The minister is not related to the men and women in the community in which he lives simply as an individual to other individuals. He is the leader of a Christian congregation which as such sustains relations to the community life. He is not simply responsible for helping individual men and women whom he can influence into the Christian life. He is responsible for associating his fellow Christians with himself in work for the Christianization of the community.

What does it mean to Christianize a community? It means to permeate all its relationships with the spirit of Jesus Christ. It means to make its members Christian in their political relations as officeholders, politicians, and voters; in their economic relations as employers and employees, as producers and investors and promoters; in their social relations as entertainers and entertained; in their educational relations as teachers and taught. It means that in each of these complicated relationships with all their many-sided contacts nothing should be done or said or planned which is not inspired by the consciousness of God's fatherly plan for his world and the determination to do what in one lies to bring that plan to realization in the community.

Now this ideal it is the function of the local church to help to realize. That is what it is for. That is the standard by which its success or failure is to be measured. If it fail here, it fails in that which is its distinctive mission. No sorrow or misfortune or sickness or suffering or sin which befalls the humblest member of the community, no selfishness or arrogance or oppression on the part of the most powerful but concerns that congregation. They are to work to make their community more Christian, and the minister should be their leader in helping them to understand what this means and how it is to be done.

[215]

How this is to be achieved in detail will differ in each particular community, for the needs of communities, like the needs of individuals, vary and no two are alike. The minister must bring to the study of his neighborhood an open mind, waiting to draw his conclusions until he has all the facts before him. He must be ready to learn from anyone who can teach him, most of all from those whom he dislikes. They, too, are parts of his parish, men and women to be won for Christ, forces that make either for good or for evil in the community, integral factors in the related units which together constitute its communal life.

But if the nature of the problem differs in each community, the motive and purpose remain the same. Our aim must be to make our Christianity socially effective, a communal as distinct from an individual possession. Only in this way can we set in motion the forces which when applied on a larger scale will result in the Christianization of the nation and of the world.

"How does the world look to you?" I asked an eminent statesman who through a life of great responsibility had had intimate acquaintance with the issues of international politics. "For the immediate present I see little that is hopeful," he answered. "But when I take the longer look, I see much."

It is with the longer look that we who are ministers are concerned. He who is building for eternity will not easily be discouraged.

CHAPTER IX

THE MINISTER AS CHURCHMAN. CHRISTIAN UNITY AND WORLD BROTHERHOOD

1. THE RESPONSIBILITY OF THE MINISTER FOR MAINTAINING CHRISTIAN STANDARDS IN THE CHURCH

2. THE SCANDAL OF OUR DIVIDED AND COMPETING CHURCHES

3. LARGER ASPECTS OF THE MOVEMENT FOR CHRISTIAN UNITY

4. THE MINISTER AS INTERPRETER OF THE CHURCH UNIVERSAL

5. A HINT FROM FOREIGN MISSIONS

6. THE KIND OF MAN THE MINISTER OUGHT TO BE

Chapter IX

1. THE RESPONSIBILITY OF THE MINISTER FOR MAINTAINING CHRISTIAN STANDARDS IN THE CHURCH

WE have passed in review the chief functions which the minister must discharge in his many-sided activity as preacher, teacher, priest, and pastor. We have seen that in whatever capacity he is functioning he has one primary responsibility: to be a witness for God to men and women who without God lack unity and direction. To a world which is torn by suspicion and distrust he brings his gospel of a love that casts out fear.

Is this all that can be said? Has the minister no more specific contribution to make to the application of Christian principles to contemporary life? He has one more contribution to make which grows out of his distinctive position as an official of the organized Church. It is his duty, so far as lies within his power, to apply the principles of Jesus Christ to that one of our human institutions for whose conduct he has primary responsibility: namely, the Christian Church.

In our previous discussion of man's dual citizenship we

[219]

pointed out the fact that what makes this dual relation so perplexing is that it is not a relation between two entirely separate and independent societies but the presence within each of the institutions to be related of two independent and conflicting principles. We have seen that it is the duty of the minister to help his parishioners to apply the principles of Christ to those aspects of institutional life which we are accustomed to call secular: the family, the school, business, the state. It is by so much more his duty to help his parishioners to apply the principles of Christ to that institution for which they are most intimately and directly responsible: the Church.

And yet I am sure you will agree with me that that application is being made very imperfectly today. As the institution committed to the proclamation of the Christian gospel we should expect the Church to apply to the conduct of its own affairs a standard higher than that which obtains in the surrounding community. And yet the fact is that in all such matters as wages, salaries, hours, and conditions of employment the competitive principle obtains in the Church as remorselessly as in any secular institution.

Take, for example, the most obvious illustration that lies at hand, the matter of ministers' salaries. A recent study shows that the salary of some ministers in the United States, even in the larger denominations, is as low as $600, and that unemployment among ministers is acute.[1] Yet when it is suggested that the principle of the minimum

[1] Brown, W. Adams, *The Education of American Ministers* (New York, 1934), Vol. I, pp. 33, 34.

wage, which is being widely recognized as an essential step in the improvement of economic conditions, be applied to ministers' salaries and that the Church as a whole assume responsibility for finding a solution of the problem of ministerial unemployment, the difficulties met have with a few notable exceptions proved thus far insuperable.[2]

Still more unsatisfactory are the conditions which affect the status of those who serve the church in other capacities, as janitor, sexton, caretaker, etc. These unordained church workers do not come under the provisions of the Social Security Act, and lack even the protection afforded to ministers by the various denominational pension funds.

When we pass from the field of economic relations to that of race we find a similar acceptance of conventional standards. Take, for example, the attitude of many Christian churches in refusing to admit negroes to membership in the same church with whites. A student of history can understand, even though he may find it difficult to approve, the principle of race segregation as practiced in certain parts of our own country. But when that principle is carried into the Church the matter becomes more serious. By what right can we criticize the caste system of India or the attitude of Hitler to the Jews when we ourselves organize our congregations on the principle of race and even in some of our church assemblies refuse to draw the natural

[2] The Methodist Church alone has recognized this responsibility on any adequate scale so far as unemployment is concerned; but so far as I know no adequate attempt has been made by any great church in this country to apply the principle of the minimum wage to its own ministers, although in several of the larger denominations (e.g., the Methodist, the Presbyterian, and the Congregational) the matter is being considered and plans proposed.

consequences of the principle of Christian brotherhood in which we say we believe?

These examples, taken at random, make it clear that so far as industrial and social relations are concerned the churches have thus far felt little responsibility for applying to the conduct of their own affairs a standard any higher than that of the surrounding community. Yet surely a church which professes to have a gospel for society as well as for the individual ought to feel a special responsibility for seeing that in the field for which it is primarily respon- sible—namely, the conduct of its own institutional life— it should give an example of the application of the prin- ciples for which it stands.

No doubt when we attempt to deal concretely with these difficulties we find ourselves involved in many perplexing questions. For the church, considered as an institution, is not something which can be isolated from the social en- vironment in which it is placed, but by the very fact that it is an institution is played upon by all the influences, na- tional and international alike, by which social standards are determined.

If then we accept our responsibility for applying Chris- tian standards to the Church, it cannot be as an isolated and independent thing, but as an experiment station in that wider process of social readjustment to which our very calling as Christians commits us.

In the attempt to deal successfully with this difficult and responsible work the laymen of the churches have a special responsibility. No charge is made more frequently against the minister than that his calling unfits him for dealing with economic and industrial questions. Let the minister stick to his preaching, and let the business man manage the business of the Church. Before the business man can expect the minister to take this suggestion seriously he must give more evidence than he has yet done of his readiness to accept responsibility for bringing his special knowledge and experience to bear in reaching a Christian solution of the problems before the Church. There are individuals and groups here and there who are doing this with conspicuous success. But on the whole it cannot be said that the Christian laymen of America have begun to face in any adequate way the opportunity which opens before them.[3]

2. THE SCANDAL OF OUR DIVIDED AND COMPETING CHURCHES

These weaknesses in the conduct of the Church as an institution are the reflection of a deeper failure—namely, our failure to realize in all its reach and sweep the brotherhood for which Christ has made us free. This failure appears most unmistakably in the fact that the Church, which holds up to mankind the ideal of a universal brotherhood, is itself divided into denominations and schools, many of which have no more relation to one another than the Jews to the Samaritans.

Wherever we look we are confronted with the fact of a divided church, and nowhere more flagrantly than in the

[3] One suggestion made to me by a Southern layman seems to me worthy of serious consideration. "Why should there not be in each city," he asked, "a council of Christian laymen, one or more from each church to study economic and social conditions in the light of Christian principles and point out in what ways the influence of the Church as a whole can wisely be used to effect improvement?"

country churches of our own land. You do not need me to multiply illustrations, for your own experience will supply them: communities scarcely large enough to support a single well-staffed church in which there are two, three, sometimes six or eight competing congregations. And you know how the efforts of our Home Boards to deal with the situation are thwarted by the attachment of the people to old habits or the unwillingness of those who have been leaders in a small church to take a subordinate position in a larger one. One is reminded of the remark of an old farmer to whom such a merger was proposed, who explained his refusal by asking whether any man in his senses would be willing to exchange the sole ownership of one mule for a share in the best race horse that you could offer him.

Our European fellow Christians are apt to account for the overchurching of America by some incurable fondness of our people for denominationalism. The fact is, of course, that it is the European churches which are primarily responsible for the multiplicity of our American denominations. Colonial America, as was to be expected in a pioneer civilization, was settled by people of adventurous disposition. They had come to the new world to find scope for self-development and self-expression which had been denied to them in the old world. This disposition was reflected in the character of their institutions, political and religious. Some of the Colonists had been members of established churches in the mother country and so accepted the principle of establishment as natural, though they might differ as to the form that establishment should take.

Others had been members of minority groups and had come to the new world for freedom to worship God according to their conscience. Protestants and Catholics, Lutherans and Reformed, Episcopalians and Presbyterians, Congregationalists and Methodists, Baptists and Quakers, lived side by side in a country whose policy toward the institutions of religion was still to be developed.

This original diversity was intensified in the later history by the continual stream of immigrants pouring into the country. These, like their predecessors of the colonial period, brought their own religious habits and traditions and did not fit easily into the structure of the existing ecclesiastical life. With their coming the number of new denominations increased and the task of achieving unity grew more complicated. Had there been a generally accepted system of education for the Protestant ministry, this difficulty might have been overcome; but the attempts of the early colonists to create such a system by the founding of colleges like Harvard and Yale failed because of the suspicion of heresy under which some of their teachers fell. To counteract this danger independent seminaries were established, and the foundation of our present system of denominational religious education was laid.

But however we account for the fact historically, the result is disastrous. It means that when we approach the difficult questions of adjustment to which this book is devoted, we have no consensus of opinion to express, no authoritative voice to represent us. Nowhere does this disunity have more disastrous effects than in our educational system. When, rightly, as I believe, we criticize our colleges and universities for the small place they give to religion in their courses of instruction, they point to us for their excuse, "When you yourselves come together and tell us what is the Christiantiy you wish us to teach our students, we will be willing to give you a hearing."

This impression of a divided church is accentuated when we leave our own country and include in our survey the other branches of the Christian Church. It acquires an almost poignant intensity when we leave Europe and America and study the new churches that are growing up against the background of the great pagan civilizations of China, India, and Japan. How can we expect the Japanese Christians to maintain their independence against the demands of the government for worship at the Shinto shrines, when they have themselves inherited all the divisions of the Western church from which they first received their gospel? Whatever inward divisions there may be among the adherents of the new secular gospels which challenge Christianity in our own day, at least they present a united front to the world. What chance is there for us to commend our doctrine of the one God when we who profess to be his children are ourselves divided?

3. LARGER ASPECTS OF THE MOVEMENT FOR CHRISTIAN UNITY

It is against this background that we must set the movement for Christian unity. That movement has two aspects, corresponding to the two meanings of the Christian Church. It is in the first place a spiritual movement, an effort to make more vivid in consciousness the great convictions and experiences which in fact make the Church one. It is in the second place a practical movement, the effort to furnish those who are conscious of their unity in Christ with organs through which they can function effectively.

Of the two, the first is incomparably the most important. Unless there is unity of experience and conviction, outward unity will carry us a very little way. Indeed it may conceivably do more harm than good. We have every reason therefore to be thankful for the growing insight that, in spite of all outward differences, there is a common Christian heritage which makes Christians in fact one.

This common heritage appears in all phases of Christian life and experience. It appears in the realm of thought. Christians of whatever name share a spiritual interpretation of the universe. Widely as they may differ in their view of the method of God's working, they believe in a Creative Spirit, whose existence gives meaning to the world and whose will sets the standard for right living. They believe that this God has revealed himself in Jesus Christ, not only as Judge, but as Saviour, not only as Creator, but as Redeemer. They believe that he is present in the world by his Holy Spirit and that he is guiding mankind through sin and suffering to the consummation of the redeemed society which faith knows as the Kingdom of God.

This common heritage appears further in the character of the Church's worship. It is at this point that the differences between Christians are most apparent. It is all the more important therefore that we should keep clearly in mind what as Christians we have in common.

To appreciate the extent of this agreement we may take the ordinary Protestant service and analyze it into its elements. First of all there are the hymns. And when we ask who wrote these hymns and who have used them, we find that we have passed all denominational lines and entered the realm of the Church universal. Catholics and Protestants, liberals and conservatives, high-churchmen and evangelicals, have all contributed to the hymns we sing in our weekly worship.

Like the hymns we sing, the prayers we pray have their roots in the worship of the older churches. More and more our Protestant churches are appropriating the treasures of devotion laid up for them in the historic liturgics. More and more we are realizing that however much we may differ in our interpretation of doctrine, in the life of prayer we feel at one.

And so I might run through the whole service and everywhere find illustrations of my theme. The Bible is the possession of no single body of Christians, but the common textbook of us all. The institution of preaching is another common possession. Most striking of all, in spite of the differences of interpretation and practice, is the persistence in the most widely diverse branches of the Church of the two symbolic acts we call sacraments: Baptism and the Supper of our Lord.

Underlying creed and liturgy, giving them meaning and significance, is a common experience. Through Christ, Christians have found peace with God and received pardon from their sin. Giving its tone to all Christian worship, public and private, the last petition uttered at night, the first prayer offered in the morning, is the prayer of the publican: "God be merciful to me a sinner." [4] And with the experience of sin Christians share also the experience of victory over sin. Through Christ they have been convicted of sin. Through Christ they have found a way of escape from sin, so that they can say with the Apostle: "Where sin abounded, grace did much more abound." [5]

This experience of forgiveness gives the Christian life its distinctive character. It is a life of adoration, of thanksgiving, of freedom, of fellowship, of hope, and of joy. Not all Christians share this fellowship to the same degree, nor is it at all times equally vivid. But when we study the lives of the greatest Christians, to whatever church they belong, we find that these qualities are present to a degree that convinces every unprejudiced observer that something radical and significant has happened that makes them akin.

With the mention of the greatest Christians we reach our most impressive illustration of Christian unity. The saints belong exclusively to no denomination or school. They are the common possession of the Church as a whole, and wherever Christian faith blossoms into holy life, there we find Christians of whatever name responding in gratitude and appropriating as their own the gift which God has given them in this evidence of his transforming grace.

But it is not enough to recognize our existing spiritual unity. We must provide it with appropriate organs of expression. And here we touch the other side of the movement for Christian unity, that which has for its ob-

[4] Luke 18: 13.   [5] Romans 5: 20.

ject the union, or at least the federation for united action, of the existing Christian denominations.

This movement has many phases. It meets us in the local community in the movement for a community church. It meets us in the nation in the development of co-operative agencies like the Federal Council of the Churches of Christ in America. It meets us on a nation-wide scale in the movement for the reunion of denominational families, and the still more ambitious World Conference on Faith and Order. Inspiring this movement in all its different phases is the conviction that if Christians are really one, that unity ought to appear in action as well as in word, and that the only effective way to convince mankind that the brotherhood which we hold up to all is a practicable ideal is to provide at least one society on a world-wide scale in which it is realized in fact.

4. THE MINISTER AS INTERPRETER OF THE CHURCH UNIVERSAL

This sets the minister his task as Christian. It is to become interpreter to his people of the unity of the Church of Christ. It is his privilege to remind them that the life they are living in their own particular communion, whether it be Baptist or Methodist or Presbyterian as the case may be, is itself but a part of that larger life which is shared by all those who love our Lord and Saviour Jesus Christ and have given themselves to his service.

There was a time when it was possible for the Christian minister to be content to know only his own church and to be ignorant of what concerned his fellow Christians of other denominational names. But today such ignorance is inexcusable. Too great interests are at stake to make such a provincial point of view any longer tolerable. With every passing year the ties which unite Christians are felt to be stronger than the interests which divide. Where the tension between the nations is becoming more acute with every passing year it is unthinkable that the churches should remain any longer apart. If the world is to be won for Christ and his Kingdom established among men, it must be by the Church, not by the churches.

But that there may be a church adequate to so august a mission we must first understand the churches. It is not enough for a man to be a Presbyterian or a Methodist. He must know what it means to be an Episcopalian or a Baptist or a Lutheran or a Congregationalist. The more remote the type of our neighbor's Christianity from our own, the less congenial its forms of expression may be to our own taste, the more we ought to desire to understand what it means to him, for it is only on the basis of an understanding of differences that we can hope to come together.

Nothing is more surprising to one who has followed with any care the movement for church unity than the extraordinary misconceptions that ministers have of the beliefs and ideals of their fellow ministers of other communions. Either they assume agreement where differences exist, or they exaggerate differences which are in fact unimportant and negligible. The minister who would lead his people intelligently must know the differences that exist between Christians and the reasons for them. He must distinguish between those permanent differences of temperament or of conviction which have maintained themselves through history and seem destined to continue indefinitely, and those temporary disagreements on which compromise is possible. He must realize that in an institution as ancient and many-sided as the Christian Church, unity does not necessarily mean uniformity, that in the Church as in the nation there is room within the larger and all-embracing unity for many lesser, relatively independent unities, and be careful not to confuse preference for the second with loyalty to the first.

Take, for example, the contrast between the type of institutional religion represented by a high-church Episcopalian of the sacramentarian and ritualistic kind, and the convinced individualist who regards baptism as the sign and seal of a preceding independent work of God's Spirit in the heart of man. How impossible it seems for Christians of these two types to understand each other. How easy for the Baptist to say of the Episcopalian, "O, well! He's an Episcopalian. You can't do business with him." How often we find the Episcopalian dismissing the Baptist as one who is altogether outside the Church as he understands it, and therefore one with whose religious vagaries he has no concern. How unconscious each, that the other represents a permanent type of religious experience reaching back into the most distant past, manifesting itself in the most different forms, persisting through all changes of intellectual belief and outward environment, appealing to something deep-seated and fundamental in human nature itself. How futile to hope for progress toward the larger

[232]

and better church for which we long till something happens in the mind and heart of each of these convinced, if narrow, Christians—something that breaks down the middle wall of partition which tradition, or prejudice, or personal preference, or it may be simple inertia, has built up between them, and makes each visualize the other for what he is, a fellow Christian for whom the Master has a use, a member of the company of his disciples—the custodian for the Church as a whole of aspects of Christian faith and experience which, but for his loyalty, narrow and misguided as may often have been the form of its expression, had been in danger of being lost altogether.

The minister then, I repeat, must know the differences between the churches, but he must know also the efforts that are being made to transcend these differences and to translate into appropriate institutional form the spiritual unity which already exists among Christians. This, too, is a long and fascinating story, deserving far more attention than it has yet received. It is a story which bears directly upon the practical tasks which concern every local congregation, for it defines the goal toward which it should move and the methods it should employ to reach it. Yet how many ministers are there who have really followed the movement for the reunion of the churches in all its complicated ramifications and would be able to discriminate intelligently between the different forms of union, organic, federal, and administrative, and their different manifestations, local, regional, national, and international? How many have followed what their own denominational agencies have contributed toward common action by the different churches in the missionary enterprise to which they are all alike committed? How many are in a position to interpret to their own people the principles and the methods by which union when it comes is to be attained?

How many know the facts of the case, the mere story of what has actually been done and planned? How many can even name the different organizations that are working for the unity of the churches? Who could give us an intelligent account of the origin and work of the Federal Council, of the Home Missions Council, of the Foreign Missions Conference, of the International Council of Religious Education, of the Council of Church Boards, of the Commission on Faith and Order, not to speak of the many movements for federation in village, city, and state?

How many know the philosophy of the movement for unity, the different principles and ideals which these different organizations represent? How many have thought their way through the complicated questions which arise when one tries to distinguish between unity and union, or between uniformity and union? Above all, how many can explain to us the different conceptions of the Church which have emerged in the course of the discussion and can point out the true affinities which unite and separate their advocates?

Finally, how many know what is being done for union in their own denomination and in their own state, and have taken such part in co-operative endeavor within their own community that they can speak out of their own experience of what is at present practicable and what must be postponed to the more distant future?

Yet all this falls within the sphere of the minister's duty as pastor. To understand Christianity he must know not only its message to the individual, he must understand the function of the Church in human affairs and know what prospect there is of its fulfilling its divinely appointed mission of being the agent for establishing the Kingdom of God on earth. Above all, he must be willing to do in his own church and in his own community the things that need to be done now.

5. A HINT FROM FOREIGN MISSIONS

What, it may be asked in conclusion, is the chance that the needed co-operation will be forthcoming? When one considers the extent of the territory to be covered, the strength and persistence of old habits of denominational and congregational loyalty, the comparatively few people who have taken to heart their responsibility for achieving a united church, it is easy to be discouraged and to regard the hope of effective unity as an idle dream.

But that is no more true of the movement for Christian unity than of any other movement which has emerged from modest beginnings and fought its way to a triumphant success.

Let us take, for example, that central object of the Church's co-operative activity, foreign missions. There was a time in which the non-Christian world was an unknown country to most Christians, and what is more, a country for whose welfare and happiness they felt no responsibility. The movement for foreign missions, like the movement for church unity, was at first the exclusive interest of a few zealous spirits. These pioneers in what was then an unknown country met with many an obstacle. They were decried as visionaries and fanatics. Sermons were preached against them. And even when they succeeded in making their way to the field of their labors, they had often to wait years before making a single convert. To a Carey or a Judson, could his vision have spanned the century to come, the present interest of the Church in foreign missions would have seemed too good to be believed.

How has this change come about? By organization. Those who believed in foreign missions founded societies to work for that end. And at first they had no official standing in the Church. They were groups of individuals who founded associations like the Y.M. and Y.W.C.A. But in time they made their case and the Church as a whole adopted their cause as its own. With the formation of national boards of missions an educational work began which carried the cause into the local congregation, and in due time made foreign missions one of the recognized interests of the entire Church.

Why should the same not be true of our movement for Christian unity? At present it is the interest of individuals and groups within the Church. Has not the time come when we should have national boards of co-operation and unity with the same dignified standing as that which we give to our boards of missions, home and foreign? Or if that seem a wasteful way of dealing with the matter, why should we not commit to our existing boards as a definite responsibility the promotion of Christian unity and the initiation of an educational campaign that shall make it as much the responsibility of the local congregation as home and foreign missions are now?

Indeed what could be a more natural outgrowth of the missionary movement than just such a development? Missions was born of faith in the universality of the Christian message and today, of all the branches of the Church universal, that in the foreign field is the most advanced in its devotion to the cause. Already the young Christians of China and India are asking why they need to perpetuate in their rising churches the divisions that have grown out of Western controversies and have lost their meaning for the churches of the farther East. By what right do we seek to bind the freedom of the Divine Spirit as he works out new ways for the transmission of his grace to the peoples who need it?

The fact is—and it is high time that we realized it—that our conventional distinction of home and foreign missions has long become obsolete. There is but one Christianity, whether at home or abroad, and all the world is a mission field—America and England, no less than China and the Islands of the Sea. It is our own paganism, we are coming to see, our own imperfect application of the principles of the gospel that has been responsible for the rise of the rival gospels to whose story much of these studies has been devoted. There is only one way in which we can successfully meet the competition of these new evangelists, and that is to take our own gospel more seriously. It is not enough to perpetuate our own imperfect and half-Christian Church. We must appropriate what is good and true in the rival faiths and show that in our own faith we can make place for it in a more complete and satisfying form.

Here, too, we have much to learn from the experience of our foreign missionaries. When they first came to the lands they wished to help it was with the conviction that they possessed the whole truth and the peoples they came to convert were wholly in error. They have long ago learned their mistake. In all the great religions God has been at work. In no country has he left himself without a witness. Wise missionaries therefore begin by recognizing the truth that those whom they would win already possess, and building upon that the superstructure of Christian faith. They preach Christ not as destroyer simply, or chiefly, but as fulfiller. Their spirit is that of Paul's address on Mars' Hill: "Whom ye ignorantly worship, him declare I unto you." [6]

It is in the same spirit that we must deal with the new pagan religions that challenge the Church today. They, too, are not wholly evil, but the reaffirmation of elements in our own gospel which we have allowed to fall into neglect. Only when we do full justice to all the truth and good they contain can we hope to win their adherents to what we believe is our larger and more satisfying faith.

So from whatever angle we approach our responsibility as ministers we are brought back at last to our need of unity. It is not a question of "either or," but of "both and." The gospel we preach is a comprehensive gospel, and for that very reason a unifying gospel. It is not a gospel for

[6] Acts 17: 23.

the individual as opposed to society, or for society as opposed to the individual, but for the individual as a member of society. It is not a gospel of flight from the world to a mystical Nirvana or content with the world to the exclusion of the hope of immortality, but a gospel that carries into each least thing done here the glory of a deathless hope. It is not a gospel that requires the sacrifice of reason in the interest of an unquestioning faith, but a gospel that uses reason as a witness to realities that are too great to be grasped by reason alone. In short, it is a gospel of the whole man, and for all time, because it is a gospel that is given by him who is more than man and who outlasts time.

It is such a gospel that we, my brothers, are charged to preach, not by word only or chiefly, but by our life, the gospel of a God who is present in history as judge and as redeemer and who through Jesus Christ is pointing the way to that better life of which up to the present we have only glimpses and foretastes.

6. THE KIND OF MAN THE MINISTER OUGHT TO BE

So I am brought to the point to which the whole course of our thought has been converging, which is this: that what the Church is to be in its ministry to the need of our time will depend in the last analysis, under God, upon what we who are its ministers make it.

It is no easy or unimportant task, my brothers, to which I summon you. It is no less than the remaking of the world through the remaking of the Church which is its servant. Who, you may well ask, is sufficient for these things? Who, may I add, would be content with a task for which he felt himself sufficient?

What power is there of mind or heart or will but this our work can use to the full? We are to be men of the world and men of God, and both of these together. As men of the world we need an open mind—alertness to catch each new breath which is blowing in the thought of our time. We must be readers not only of the books of those with whom we agree but of those with whom we differ. But it is not what we read that matters, but how. We must be thinkers, bringing our own fresh judgment to bear upon each new question that is brought to us, and content when no immediate answer is forthcoming to wait for the riper wisdom still to be given. Above all, we must be friends, eager to believe the best in every man we touch, making him feel that our wider vision has lent us sympathy even when it leads us to critical judgment.

Yes, we are to be men of the world, in the broadest and best sense of that term. But we are to be men of God as well, and that means men of prayer, humble, patient, reverent, but withal courageous, joyful, carrying into every situation in life the tonic of an unconquerable faith.

It is for such men as these that the world is looking and there is no limit to what they can do for it when they are found. I congratulate you, my brothers, on your high calling, and pray God that he may give you grace to be the leaders our time needs.

INDEX

INDEX

Abraham, 77
Action Populaire, 201
Alabama, Black Belt of, 206
Alma Mater, 96
America, 180, 226, 237; church and state in contemporary, 17, 42; over-churching of, 224; Roman Catholic Church in, 42, 43
American, Christianity, 114; churches, 18
Americans, 181
Ames, E. S., 97
Amos, 149
Anglicans, 174
Apologetics, Christian, 71
Armaments, limitation of, 34
Armistice, 25
Artist's belief in an ideal world of beauty, 74
Assyria, 147
Assyrians, 151
Augustine, Saint, belief in God, 83
Austria, 149
Authority, breakdown of, 28

Baptism, 228
Baptist, 225, 230, 231, 232; Church, 17
Baptist General Association of Virginia, 164
Bennett, John C., 189
Bible, 45, 141, 180, 182, 228; accepted by Protestants as divine revelation, 43, 44; as revelation, 16; God speaks through, 127-129; opposition to compulsory reading of, 164
Bishop of Rome, 175
Black Belt of Alabama, 206
Boston, 181
Briggs, Charles A., 53
Brooks, Phillips, belief in God, 83
Brown, Arthur J., 179
Bucharin, N., 99
Buddhism, 146

Caesar, 32
Calvary, 154
Calvin, John, 76
Calvinists, 142
Canaan, 147
Carey, 236
Carmelite, 189
Catholic interpretation of history, 141, 142
Catholicism, Roman and Anglican, 114; teaching in, 163
Catholics, 225
Centralia riots, study of, 202
Chamber of Commerce of the United States, 53
Chaplaincy, study of the, 202
Chicago, 181
China, 226, 237; boatman, 144
Chinese church, 118
Christ, see Jesus
Christendom, passing of, 30-35
Christian, church as subject of teaching, 173-181; convictions concerning God in history, 150-157; gospel as subject of teaching, 170-173; unity, 226-230
Christianity, 148; religion of minority in whole countries, 18; subject of teaching, 166-170
Church, aid to minister in application of Christian principles, 199-207; and Kingdom, connection between, 178, 179; as revelation, 16; crisis one of transfer of loyalties to the state, 32-35; definition of function of, 63, 64; divided and competitive, 223-226; God speaks through, 127-129; in Czarist Russia, 89, 90; new factors in world facing, 27-32; only institution whose specialty is worship, 25; responsibility for maintaining Christian standards, 219-223; theologian's definition of, 17; universal, 230-235; what holds in trust,

INDEX

Gladstone, W. E., 131

God, 40, 58, 70; arguments for the being of, 71-74; as wonder-worker, 120; belief in, 82, 83; comradeship with, 118; consciousness, loss of in contemporary religion, 111-114; devotion to common good a substitute for, 94-99; difference in, 115; difficulties in realizing presence of, 119-123; discovery of, 115; Fatherhood of, 55; found in better self, 124-127; found in great traditions of race, 124-130; found in nature, 63-84, 122, 123; found in person of Jesus Christ, 124-131; how to make real, 109-135; humanist's substitute for, 87-106; in history, 139-157; intellectual argument against belief in, 65-84; moral argument against belief in, 87-91; mystery in, 115, 116; proposed substitutes for, 63-106; scientist's substitute for, 63-84; self-expression a substitute for, 91-94; speaks through Bible, 127-129; speaks through Church, 127-129; supreme object of devotion, 117; the ultimate reality, 115; where found, 123-131

Good, common, a substitute for God, 94-99

Gospel, Christian, 57, 58; of blood and soil, 31; of dictatorships, 57, 58

Great Britain, 164

Greece, 168

Harvard University, 164, 225

Hinduism, 146

Hitler, 31, 57, 102, 103, 106, 118, 221

Hocking, W. E., 134

Holy Spirit, 46, 141, 227

Home Boards, 224

Home Missions Council, 234

Human institutions, spiritual meaning of, 19-21

Human solidarity, 154-157

Humanist's substitute for God, 87-106

Hymns, 228

Independence Day, 20

India, 157, 226, 237; caste system of, 221; new national church of, 169

Information Service, 202

International Council of Religious Education, **234**

Isaiah, 77, 149

Islands of the Sea, 237

Israel, 143, 144, 151, 153, 168; prophets of, 145, 146; religion of, **146, 147**

Israelites, 151

Italians, 98, 102, 181

Italy, 103; church and state in, 32

James, William, 69

Japan, 29, 119, 157, 207, 226; church and state in, 32; church of, 169

Jeremiah, 149

Jerusalem, 142, 143

Jesus, 40, 45, 58, 59, 77, 227; as a humanist, 101; as a Teutonic chieftain, 31; belief in God, 83; God found in person of, 124-131; as God's supreme self-revelation, 129

Jews, **168, 221**

Judge, 227

Judson, 236

Kagawa, Toyohiko, 119, 157, 207

Kant, Immanuel, 72, 73

Kingdom of God, 142, 143, 148, 170, 173, 193, 227, 231, 235; and church, connection between, 178, 179

Latimer, 156

Lawrence, Brother, 25

League of Nations, 51, 152, 211, 212

Link, Henry C., **113**

Lisieux, St. Thérèse of, 189

Lord's Supper, 228

Lothian, Lord, 104, 105

Loyola, St. Ignatius, 134

Ludendorff, Frau, 31

[245]

INDEX